WHY CORPORATIONS FAIL

Other Books By Lawrence C. Gambone

The Dilution of America (with Louis C. Gilde)

WHY CORPORATIONS FAIL

A PRIMER FOR THE DYSFUNCTIONAL CORPORATION

Lawrence C. Gambone

CreateSpace On-Demand Publishing, LLC.
© 2014 By Lawrence C. Gambone
Printed in the United States of America

96 95 94 93 92 91 90 89   10 9 8 7 6 5

ISBN-13: 978-1494344221
ISBN-10: 149434422X

As with any written work, there are a number of people who helped me put this primer together; and this is the place to thank them.

First on the list is my wife, Marilyn, who is critical of everything I write. So, when I showed her the first draft, I braced myself for a disparaging review. She liked it. Next is my friend Andrew Butrica, PhD, who helped me immensely with editing and writing. And last but not least is, Lou Gilde, who argued profusely with me about some of my "fixations" while writing the primer.

TABLE OF CONTENTS

If you can't make it good, at least make it look good.
— Bill Gates

Table of Contents

PROLOGUE

Blessed is he who expects nothing, for he shall never be disappointed.
— Alexander Pope

PRIMER

The reader should know why I am calling this book a "primer." The Merriam-Webster Dictionary defines "Primer" as a noun, chiefly British that comes from the "Middle English for a layperson's prayer book," which, in turn comes from "Anglo-French, from Medieval Latin *primarium,* from Late Latin, neuter of *primarius* primary." The first known use of "primer" dates to the 14th century.

The dictionary listed the following definitions for "primer:"

> 1: a small book for teaching children to read
> 2: a small introductory book on a subject
> 3: a short informative piece of writing

Obviously, I am assuming that you know how to read; therefore, definitions 2 and 3 are the ones that I am utilizing here—this is a "small introductory book" on the subject; and it is (I hope) an "informative piece of writing."

My intent, in this small introductory book, is to provide you with a unique way of looking at today's large corporations and the small corps of executive personnel who run them. The basic concepts that I am presenting are neither complicated nor difficult to understand. Hopefully, they shed a glimmer of light on the many complicated and varied reasons for the disastrous corporate collapses that took place during the first decade of the 21st century.

And finally, as you read the book, I hope you will come to the conclusion that what I say makes sense.

Lawrence C. Gambone
March 2014

INTRODUCTION

WHY DO CORPORATIONS FAIL?

I can calculate the motion of heavenly bodies, but not the madness of people.
— **Isaac Newton**

There are many reasons why corporations fail. They succumb to external forces, such as economic downturns; fail to invent or reinvent products that reflect consumer interests; make ill-timed investments; or, most likely, they yield to a combination of circumstances. But, every corporate collapse contains one key factor in addition to these conditions: The company falls prey to internal problems—it is dysfunctional.

I remember the first time I came across the term "dysfunctional." It was many years ago in a magazine article. It was used to portray a family psychologically, and it replaced the stronger, more primitive "neurotic" as the descriptive adjective.

I liked the word immediately. I recall thinking at the time that it was much more encompassing but far less declarative than "neurotic." For me, the word "dysfunctional" embraced neuroses, added an inability to cope, while at the same time lessened the impact of inherent mental instability.

The subject magazine article had used the new word to describe a "nuclear family;" that is, daddy, mommy, and their exasperating offspring. The term seemed to catch on quite quickly. I believe it provided a revelation for most people. Rather than refer to themselves or their nuclear units by the negative, arcane term "neurotic," they could advance now to the more progressive "dysfunctional."

It was a perceptual "jump-up" if not a virtual one. And it had an unforeseen result: suddenly, belonging to a dysfunctional, rather than a neurotic, family encompassed not only fewer stigmas, but engendered in actuality some small status.

It's easy to see how this happened. No one wants to be perceived as being neurotic. The term evokes negative aspects of mental deficiencies that generally will cause others to avoid us. However, in this enlightened age we all can have some form of selective dysfunction with minimal fear of becoming socially ostracized. I mean nobody's perfect, right? And we all should be permitted certain minor failures or eccentricities, right?

Thus, "dysfunctional" came into its own as the reigning descriptive adjective for non-functioning or semi-functioning individuals and families. Very simply, the term makes us human. In fact, our dysfunction, by making us all a little more human, may serve even as a common bond.

But, can the term "dysfunctional" be expanded to describe not only individuals and the "nuclear family," but also the much larger, less nuclear, "corporate family?" Well, it makes sense when you think about it.

We would be hard pressed to understand the meaning of a "neurotic corporation." The term by far is too negative, too narrow, and fails to project the inherent emotional and intellectual instability factors in a manner broad enough to define adequately something as complex as a corporation. The word neurotic is just a bit too personal.

But, describing a corporation as dysfunctional is more accurate, understandable in its entirety, and hopefully, acceptable intellectually. This is because the negative, neurotic aspect of the entity's defining adjective has been removed.

THE DYSFUNCTIONAL CORPORATION

All corporations have some form of dysfunction. It is a basic law of nature—nothing is perfect. However, having a "form of dysfunction" does not mean that a company truly is dysfunctional; nor does it mean the company is doomed to fail. As I will point out in this primer, "truly dysfunctional" corporations are rare. They are organizations that display from the very top of their hierarchies a lack of honesty, integrity, and ethics while dealing with the business world and to some extent even their own employees.

There are untold reasons why corporations are dysfunctional; and, of course, each corporation will have its own story. Nevertheless, in this primer I will address three major causal determinants for corporate dysfunction:

1) The structure of the corporation encompasses dysfunction;
2) The basic principles that govern the corporation are dysfunctional in themselves; and
3) The members of the corporation, being human, are dysfunctional by definition.

In general, the determinants described in category 1) apply to all corporations. This is because all corporate entities are structured functionally, legally, and historically pretty much in the same way.

The principles and dysfunctions described in category 3) apply also to all entities. People are people. And in the case of this causal determinant, it is merely the magnitude of the dysfunction that makes the difference.

It is the key factors described in category 2) that will separate the "men from the boys," the "good from the bad," or the "yin from the yang," if you will pardon my rhetorical expressions. If a company's governing principles are not based on a sound footing of ethics, integrity, and honesty, the company is doomed to dysfunction.

COROLLARY: All corporations have some form of dysfunction—it is a basic law of nature—nothing is perfect.

For the purposes of this treatise, we are interested in corporations that are large, multi-faceted conglomerates only. It is these companies that possess the required characteristics for dysfunction: Large-scale economic activity supported by large sums of invested capital.

PART I

THE DYSFUNCTIONAL CORPORATE STRUCTURE

THE DYSFUNCTIONAL CORPORATE STRUCTURE

Capitalism is the legitimate racket of the ruling class.
— Al Capone

Many Americans possess an unenlightened view of the corporation, seeing it as a modern form of "social organization" charged with a dynamic mission and with operations that are based on modern financing, efficient production techniques, and (since most corporations are owned by shareholders) the democratic principles of our great nation.

Simply put, corporations embrace capitalism; and capitalism is America. Well, unfortunately, patriotism notwithstanding, nothing could be farther from the truth.

First of all, you have to understand that the "modern corporation" really isn't so modern. In actuality, the basic structure of the corporation dates back to the Middle Ages. Thus, the concept of the modern corporation with its stockholders, executive management, modern production processes, and extraordinary financing schemes is misplaced—rather, these are just contemporary revisions to a very old structure.

The world's oldest industrial corporation still in operation is Sweden's Stora Kopparberg Bergslags Aktiebolag—and I will admit that I never heard of it until I started research for this primer.

Chartered in 1347 by King Magnus Eriksson to organize the country's copper miners, Stora Kopparberg began formal operations a mere 73 years after King John signed the Magna Carta and nearly 150 years before Columbus discovered . . . or, to be more accurate, I should say "traveled to" . . . America. Stora Kopparberg's formal organization as a company made Sweden the major supplier of copper to all of Europe. The company continued in that endeavor until the 17th century, when it began to branch out.[1]

Stora Kopparberg today is a successful conglomerate. In addition to its mining operations, it is Sweden's largest producer of electricity, one of the biggest manufacturers of pulpwood and newsprint (with exports to 40 nations), the largest supplier of dairy and agricultural produce, the biggest steelmaker, a major producer of industrial chemicals, and a large consumer paint manufacturer.

---

[1] Though formally chartered in 1347, the first mention of Stora Kopparberg is on a sheepskin parchment dated June 16, 1288, which records the following transaction: Bishop Peter of Vaesteraas, in the province of Dalacarlia, bought back a share in a copper mine which he had sold five years earlier when negotiating cash from a moneylender.

THE FEUDAL CORPORATION

Indeed, history is nothing more than a tableau of crimes and misfortunes.
— Voltaire (1694-1778)

Though it may be dynamic, the so-called modern corporation is far from democratic. Its structure dates back to the Middle Ages, and its governing principles are based on feudalism. It is, in fact, a feudal institution. Its aristocracy or lords, called "executives," dictate to the serfs or peasants, called "employees," just how their lives will go. And, like the feudal societies of the Middle Ages, the employees have no power over the operation of the corporation, do 90 percent of the work, and receive practically none of the rewards.

The corporation's royalty (i.e., executives) reap nearly all the rewards and hold all the power, including the power of life or death (in an economic sense) over their subjects. Think about it! Corporations even use the word "terminate" to describe how they unload unwanted personnel.

I'm willing to bet that at least 90% of the people who read this book have had the misfortune of being laid off at least once in their meager careers. Thus, 90% of you know the humiliation of being hauled in front of a Human Resources representative who told you that you were no longer of any worth to your (feudal) corporation and therefore were "terminated."

All your years of hard work, dedication, loyalty, and trust were disregarded blatantly by corporate royalty who did not have the courage even to preside over your demise. Instead, they relegated the task to an HR representative.

And, did you ever wonder, as I have, why that HR representative, a person who produces nothing of value to the corporation, actually was deemed to have more worth than you? Well, they do perform a service. In the Middle Ages, HR representatives were called "executioners."

And, I ask: How many executives were laid off at the time(s) you were removed forcefully from your place of employment? I'll bet you can count them on no hands.

> **COROLLARY:** All corporations are feudal institutions. It is the corporation's royalty (i.e., executives) who reap rewards and hold power, including the power of life or death (in an economic sense) over their subjects.

THE CORPORATE MISSION – A BASIC MISCONCEPTION

Be nice to nerds. Chances are you'll end up working for one.
– Bill Gates

A corporation's stated mission generally is to build something, provide a particular service, or to assist another individual or corporation with building something or providing a service. Just go on-line: most corporations will state their missions in their websites.

For example, Honda Corporation's mission statement is: "Maintaining a global viewpoint, we are dedicated to supplying products of the highest quality, yet at a reasonable price for worldwide customer satisfaction."

Dell Corporation's statement is: "To be the most successful computer company in the world at delivering the best customer experience in markets we serve."

WorldCom's mission statement as of 1998 was rather anti-climactic: "Our objective is to be the most profitable, single-source provider of communications services to customers around the world."

And my favorite, the now defunct Enron's motto was brief, direct, and entirely misleading: "Respect, Integrity, Communication and Excellence."[2]

But, those are examples of the "stated" mission. A corporation's "actual" or "virtual" mission is far different. The actual mission is covert and unspoken because the executive aristocracy do not want the peasant workers to understand the company's true purpose.

The actual mission of a corporation is to increase and protect the wealth, influence, and power of its feudal lords or executives—and if you don't think this is true then consider the following.

---

[2] Both WorldCom and Enron, of course, went bankrupt because of the fraud, deceit, and thefts that were perpetrated by executives at the very top of the corporations.

The stated mission of auto manufacturers is to "build something," that is, to manufacture automobiles. I already have pointed out that Honda is "dedicated to supplying products of the highest quality." And in times of prosperity, that's what they do; they manufacture automobiles.

However, during an economic downturn, that mission changes to its actual objective: protecting the wealth, influence, and power of the corporation's aristocracy. If this isn't true, then why did GMC, Chrysler, and Ford shut down plants, decrease production, and lay off thousands of employees during the last economic crisis?

Cars were NOT being built, and thousands of serfs . . . I mean, employees . . . were no longer employed. Nevertheless, throughout the entire downturn, corporate executives received their huge paychecks.

COROLLARY: The actual mission of a corporation is to protect and increase the wealth, influence, and power of its feudal lords or executives.[3]

We've even witnessed an infusion of billions of dollars of taxpayer money into these corporations and, in the instance of GMC, an unprecedented takeover by the federal government. Even that didn't deter the true mission of the corporation (to protect the wealth of its executives).

The equally unprecedented firing of Rick Wagoner, GMC's Chief Executive Officer (CEO), by the President of the United States may seem to evidence a need for accountability except for the fact that the ousting came with a $20 million payout package.

---

[3] The "actual" mission of a corporation includes increasing the wealth of its stockholders, too; however, for purposes of this primer, we have excluded the stockholders because they do not participate in the company's day-to-day decision-making processes.

The man was FIRED, meaning he was incompetent. He made mistakes and bad decisions. He lacked sufficient foresight to buffer his corporation from economic disaster. But, in appreciation of his failure, he received a cool $20 million.

When the average "Working Joe" is laid-off (NOT FIRED, mind you), most likely he receives a small percentage of his annual salary as a severance package. At best, this will amount to a few thousand dollars. The last time I was laid off, my severance pay barely covered a couple of mortgage payments.

EXECUTIVE COMPENSATION

Money can't buy you friends . . . . But you get a better class of enemy.
– Spike Milligan

CEO's and other high-ranking executives always have been extremely well-compensated; and in most instances deservedly so. It is not the compensation that is of concern, but rather the gross inequity of that compensation compared to the workers or employees of the executives' firms.

Executive compensation is structured usually within a contractual agreement between the executive and the corporation. Generally, it includes a base salary and "additional compensation" (bonuses, stock options, incentive payments, etc.). Additional compensation payments result from formulas based on profit or profit margin, cost reduction, or any combination of a number of factors deemed important to the corporation.

"Business Exchange" at bx.businessweek.com, informs us that:[4]

There are five basic tools to executive compensation in U.S. organizations. These are: base salary, short-term incentives, long-term incentives (LTIP), employee benefits, and perquisites. In a typical modern U.S. corporation, the CEO and other top executives are paid salary plus short-term incentives or bonuses. This combination is referred to as total cash compensation (TCC).

I contend that short-term and long-term incentives help drive executive greed. If economically killing (laying-off) a thousand employees will make the numbers better (thus increasing executive bonuses and/or other additional compensation), corporate royalty

---

[4] "Executive Compensation," Business Exchange, Blomberg.com, on-line at: http://bx.businessweek.com/executive-compensation/news/ (Accessed November 3, 2012).

will have no second thoughts about committing "socio-economic decimation."[5]

And within the last few decades, the problem—disparate income levels—has multiplied to the absolute detriment of the average worker.

On page 6 of his book, *After-Shock*, Robert B. Reich states:[6]

> *In the late 1970's, the richest 1 percent of the country took in less than 9 percent of the nation's total income. After that, income concentrated in fewer and fewer hands. By 2007, the richest 1 percent took in 23.5 percent of total national income. It is no mere coincidence that the last time income was this concentrated was in 1928.*

On November 15, 2005, Carola Frydman of Harvard University and Raven E. Saks of the Federal Reserve Board of Governors published, "Historical Trends in Executive Compensation 1936-2003."[7] In that report, the authors state:

> *The average real value of total compensation experienced three distinct phases: a sharp decline during World War II, a modest and gradual increase from the mid-1940s to the 1970s, and a high and accelerating growth rate in the 1980s and 1990s.*

The following chart, which displays average and median executive compensation compared to average worker's wages, appeared on

---

[5] The executive's rationalization of greed that allows this to happen is discussed in Part II, "The Dysfunctional Principles of a Corporation."

[6] Robert B. Reich; *After-Shock: The Next Economy and America's Future* (New York, Alfred A. Knopf, 2010).

[7] Carola Frydman and Raven E. Saks, "Historical Trends in Executive Compensation 1936-2003," November 15, 2005, on-line at: http://faculty.chicagobooth.edu/workshops/AppliedEcon/archive/pdf/FrydmanSecondPaper.pdf (Accessed November 3, 2012).

page 57 of the report. It displays the "spike" in executive compensation beginning in the 1980s.

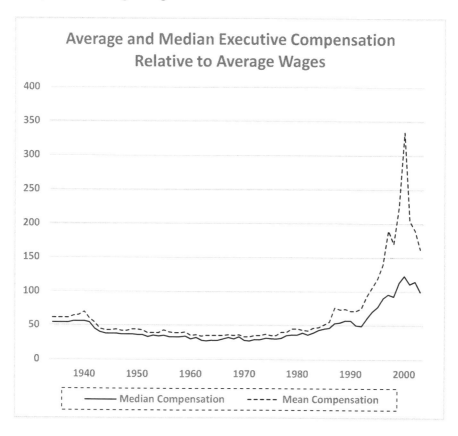

Average and Median Executive Compensation Relative to Average Wages

Note: Total Compensation is composed of salary, bonuses, long-term bonus payments, and stock option grants. Average compensation in each year is expressed relative to total wage and salary accruals per full-time equivalent employee from table 6.6 of the National Income and Product Accounts. Based on the three highest-paid officers in the largest 50 firms in 1940, 1950 and 1990.

Lawrence Mishel of the Economic Policy Institute mirrored Frydman's and Saks' findings. On June 21, 2006, he published a report entitled, "CEO-to-worker pay imbalance grows." In that report, Mishel stated:[8]

---

[8] Lawrence Mishel, "CEO-to-worker pay imbalance grows," Economic Policy Institute,

In 1965, U.S. CEOs in major companies earned 24 times more than an average worker; this ratio grew to 35 in 1978 and to 71 in 1989. The ratio surged in the 1990s and hit 300 at the end of the recovery in 2000. The fall in the stock market reduced CEO stock-related pay (e.g., options) causing CEO pay to moderate to 143 times that of an average worker in 2002. Since then, however, CEO pay has exploded and by 2005 the average CEO was paid $10,982,000 a year, or 262 times that of an average worker ($41,861).

According to Mishel, in 2005, a CEO earned on average approximately $42,238 per workday (260 workdays per year), which is more than an average worker earned in the entire work year. He included the following graphic representation (Figure A) in his article:

FIGURE A Ratio of CEO to average worker pay, 1965 - 2005

Data note: CEO pay is realized direct compensation defined as the sum of salary, bonus, value of restricted stock at grant, and other long-term incentive award payments from a Mercer Survey

Economic Snapshot, June 21, 2006, on-line at http://www.epi.org/publication/webfeatures_snapshots_20060621/ (Accessed November 3, 2012).

conducted for the *Wall Street Journal* and prior *Wall Street Journal*-sponsored surveys. Worker pay is the hourly wage of production and nonsupervisory workers, assuming the economy-wide ratio of compensation to wages and a full-time, year-round job.

The graphs support my thesis: the true mission of the corporation is to protect the wealth and power of its executive royalty. Both graphs show that in 2002, during the economic downturn, the ratio of executive compensation to employee compensation dropped. Mishel described the reduction in CEO pay from 300 to 143 as a result of the "fall in the stock market." However, I believe this does not tell the whole story.

The ratios in both graphs display a comparison of executive pay to "employee" pay. Had the graphs taken into consideration the fact that in 2002 nearly 6% of the workforce was unemployed, the ratio for that year undoubtedly would be much higher. And, it goes without saying that the ratio "exploded" back up to 262 within a mere three years.

I will cover this income disparity further when we talk about the Dysfunctional Principles of a Corporation.

COROLLARY: The average CEO earns more in one work day than the average employee earns in a full year. Executives may deserve high pay. It is not the compensation of executives that is a dysfunction, but the gross inequity of that compensation compared to the workers or employees of the executives' firms.

UNIONS – CHAMPIONS OF THE EMPLOYEES

Nature does not deceive us; it is we who deceive ourselves.
— Jean-Jacques Rousseau (1762)

I have maintained that the feudal corporation is controlled solely by its "royal" executives and that the "peasant" workers have no authority and receive minimal rewards. It could be argued, however, that through the power of their unions, employees do have a say in the operation of the corporation.

Before going any further with this, I will make the following brief disclaimer: Unions deserve much more time and thought than I am willing to give them in this primer. Tomes have been written about unions, both pro and con; and I would direct the serious reader to those manuscripts. The less serious reader should continue on to the next paragraph.

Despite their openly contentious battle with corporate management, unions, it is my opinion, actually have fallen right in step with corporations. To begin with, unions, too, are feudal in structure, dating back to the various artisan and merchant guilds created during the Middle Ages.

Today, the biggest difference between unions and corporations is in nomenclature. Union heads are called "union leaders" rather than "executives," and the serfs or peasants are called "members" rather than "workers" or "employees." But the most disconcerting characteristic of unions is the misperception of their mission by union members.

I contend that, similar to corporations, the true mission of unions is to protect and increase the wealth and power of union leaders. Unfortunately, "union members" do not understand this.

Not for one minute would employees ever believe that the executives of a corporation truly care for them. Employees are savvy. Though they may not think of the company they work for as a feudal institution, they do understand that a corporation's executives are self-serving individuals who consider employees to be expendable.

However, workers mistakenly believe that union leaders *do* care about them—a fantasy that the union leaders make no attempt to discourage. It is because workers lack a true understanding of the union as a feudal organization that they believe it exists for them and that its leaders consider them (the members) to be equals.

In my opinion, this belief is incorrect: Unions exist solely for the advancement and well-being of the union leaders. And as in any feudal institution, the nobility will provide only minimal care for the peasantry. For example, in a June 28, 2004, article, *USA Today* stated that ". . . current reporting requirements do not tell rank-and-file union members clearly how their dues are spent."[9]

Of course, union nobility would not want the peasants to know how they (the nobles) spend their (the serfs) money. That's because union leaders take action for their members on only two occasions:

a) The action will increase the leaders' notoriety, wealth, influence, and/or power
b) The action is a move to ensure that there is no decrease to the leaders' wealth, influence, and/or power.

COROLLARY: The actual mission of a union is to protect and increase the wealth, influence, and power of its feudal lords (union leaders).

---

[9] "Many union leaders earn six figures," Gannett.com, on-line at: http://www.usatoday.com/money/workplace/2004-06-28-union-heads-incomes_x.htm, (Accessed November 3, 2012).

UNION LEADERS' SALARIES

He who has lost honor can lose nothing more.
– Publilius Syrus (46 BC)

In a manner similar to corporate royalty, union leader salaries began spiking upward in the beginning of the new millennium without corresponding increases in member salaries.

According to data filed under the Labor Management Reporting and Disclosure Act (LMRDA), the number of union officials and staff earning high salaries has skyrocketed in recent years. For example, the number of individuals earning over $100,000 a year more than doubled between 2000 and 2004. Over the same period the number of officers and staff earning more than $150,000 increased 84 percent.

As an example, according to the organization's 2008 Form 990,[10] Marty Beil, Executive Director of American Federation of State, County, and Municipal Employees (AFSCME) Council 24 SEPAC (Wisconsin) made $161,847. Biel's assistant director at AFSCME 24 SEPAC, Jana Weaver, made $138,553. In fact, according to the Form 990, in 2008 all six full-time AFSCME 24 SEPAC employees made six-figure salaries.

The Associated Press appears to support the data regarding union leaders' salaries. According to a June 28, 2004, release, the average annual salary for a union president in 2003 was $122,297. But some union leaders made far more than the average. Quoting that release, *USA Today* reported on the same date:[11] "The leaders

---

[10] Form 990, *Return of Organization Exempt From Income Tax*, is the tax form filed by certain non-profit organizations under section 501(c), 527, or 4947(a)(1) of the Internal Revenue Code.

[11] "Many union leaders earn six figures," Gannett.com, on-line at: http://www.usatoday.com/money/workplace/2004-06-28-union-heads-incomes_x.htm, (Accessed November 3, 2012).

of America's labor unions are a well-paid bunch: Four earned more than $400,000 last year, and another four had salaries above $300,000."

In an article by Alan Yonan Jr., the Honolulu *Star Advertiser* reported on July 31, 2011, that, according to an analysis of data from the U.S. Labor Department and the Internal Revenue Service, "executives of the top 25 unions [in Hawaii] earned an average of $157,596 in compensation" in 2010.[12]

The article continued by stating that for Hawaii's top 25 unions: "Thirteen officials received raises, seven took pay cuts and three had no change in their compensation." Two of the officials were new to their jobs; thus, there was no comparative data. This means that 13 of Hawaii's 25 top union leaders (52%) accepted pay increases during Hawaii's "financial crunch," which resulted in most union members being laid-off, accepting pay cuts, or at best, foregoing pay raises.

On February 28, 2010, *The Record*, a Bergen County, New Jersey, newspaper reported the following salaries for the heads of the state's largest teachers union, the New Jersey Education Association (NJEA):[13]

> ***$270,000:*** *Salary of NJEA Executive Director Vincent Giordano. He also gets deferred compensation, calculated when he leaves.*

---

[12] Alan Yonan Jr., "Union leaders' salaries reflect members woes," The Honolulu *Star Advertiser*, July 31, 2011, on-line at:
http://www.staradvertiser.com/business/20110731_Union_leaders_salaries_reflect_members_woes.html?id=126449928 (Accessed November 4, 2012).

[13] Patricia Alex and Leslie Brody, "The NJEA vs. Governor Christie: Two powerhouses doing battle," *The Record*, NorthJersey.com, Behind The News, February 28, 2010, on-line at: http://www.northjersey.com/news/85754237_The_NJEA_vs__Governor_Christie__two_powerhouses_doing__battle.html (Accessed November 3, 2012).

$263,000: *Salary of NJEA President Barbara Keshishian, who also gets deferred compensation and a state pension.*

$63,111: *Average teacher pay statewide.*

COROLLARY: The average union leader's salary does not compare to that of the top earners running U.S. companies. Nevertheless, including even the few leaders who accept pay cuts, the average leader's salary greatly exceeds the average union member's pay.

Remember this the next time you pay your union dues: your union leader will receive his inordinately high salary whether you are working, marching on the picket line, or laid-off (unemployed).

PART I
THE DYSFUNCTIONAL CORPORATE STRUCTURE

IN SUMMATION

A key element in the dysfunction of a corporation or union is its feudal structure, which supports a lack of accountability and responsibility for its nobility (executives/leaders) at the expense of the health and welfare of its peasants (employees, workers, union members).

Feudalism is a basic—and faulty—building block that supports the dysfunctional corporate structure.

PART II

THE DYSFUNCTIONAL PRINCIPLES OF THE CORPORATION

THE DYSFUNCTIONAL PRINCIPLES OF THE CORPORATION

Those are my principles. If you don't like them, I have others.
— **Groucho Marx**

At the very top, all dysfunctional corporations run on two principles, and ONLY two principles: Ego and Greed. These principles are not mutually exclusive. Rather, they exist in a symbiosis that borders on the perverse. Greed and Ego totally govern the management of dysfunctional corporations to the exclusion of all other principles. This means that nothing else—for example, compassion, integrity, or (heaven forbid) ethics—enters even remotely into the picture.

GREED

Greed is traditionally viewed as being a selfish, sinful, or even evil, desire. The Catholic Church specifically cites Greed as one of the Seven Deadly Sins. St. Thomas Aquinas said that Greed is "a sin against God, just as all mortal sins, in as much as man condemns things eternal for the sake of temporal things." And even Dante Alighieri in his famous *Inferno* allocates an entire section of Hell to the painful punishment of the greedy.

Dr. Stephen Diamond, a forensic psychologist, states:[14]

> *Greed, like lust and gluttony, is traditionally considered a sin of excess .... Both greed and gluttony correspond closely with what Gautama Buddha called* desire*: an over attachment to the material world and its pleasures which is at the root of all*

---

[14] Stephen Diamond, PhD, "Is Greed Ever Good? The Psychology of Selfishness;" *Psychology Today*, March 25, 2009, on-line at: http://www.psychologytoday.com/blog/evil-deeds/200903/is-greed-ever-good-the-psychology-selfishness (Accessed November 5, 2012).

human suffering. Greed is about never being satisfied with what one has, always wanting and expecting more. It is an insatiable hunger. A profound form of gluttony.

COROLLARY: Greed is the desire to obtain something. Greed in the absolute is the desire to obtain something with a total disregard of the means, moral/ethical implications, and consequences that ensue.

EGO

This is a primer on corporate dysfunction, not a treatise on psychology. Nevertheless, individual dysfunction is an important component of corporate dysfunction, and it is for this reason that I will discuss briefly Freud's theory of personality.

Sigmund Freud (1856-1936), in his psychoanalytic theory of personality, believed that each individual's personality included three components: Id, Ego, and Superego.

According to Freud the Id is the structure of personality that contains our basic, selfish interests. We are born with the Id, it is totally unconscious, and it has no contact with reality.

The Ego can be considered to be the executive branch of the personality. It is the structure that all individuals use to make decisions.

And finally, the Superego is the component that allows us to make moral and ethical decisions and actions. It is composed of values and volitions that we attain during our formative years. Freud believed that the Superego only developed when a person reached approximately 5 years of age. It can be considered to be synonymous with the "conscience."

I have stated earlier that Ego (along with Greed) is one of the basic building blocks of the dysfunctional corporation. Ego and Greed are

34

symbiotic, that is, they feed upon each other. We use the term "Ego" because Freud believed that it was the one component that controlled the other two (the Id and Superego).

Quite simply, if the Id were allowed free reign, we all would be voracious, anti-social monsters, caring only for ourselves. If the Superego were unrestrained, we would be compulsively controlled automatons who could act, but not accept responsibility. It is the Ego that keeps the uncontrollable components of our personality in check.

I believe that the Ego can be overtaken by the Id. This corruption of the psyche's controller is an important factor. It allows corporate royalty to accept readily the "Grouping of Greed Needs."

COROLLARY: Greed and Ego are building blocks that support the dysfunctional individual, family, and corporation.

THE GROUPING OF GREED NEEDS (Greed Group)

Psychologist Abraham Maslow introduced the concept of a hierarchy of needs in a paper published in 1943 entitled, "A Theory of Human Motivation." His subsequent book, *Motivation and Personality*, expanded on the concept. Simply put, all humans have basic "needs" that must be met. Maslow believed those needs to be:

▲ Self-Actualization
  Esteem
  Love/belonging
  Safety
  Physiological

Basically, I believe this is really a hierarchy of "worry." We MUST have the physiological needs (food, water, shelter, etc.) in order to survive. But we "worry" about everything else.

Absent the basic physiological needs, all else becomes moot because, most likely, we will be dead. But, once we are fed, clothed, and sheltered, we become free to worry about our safety, who does or doesn't love us, who will or won't respect us, and what we can and can't do with our lives.

Freud's Id, Ego, and Superego, when coupled with raw greed and applied to Maslow's Needs Hierarchy, can be gathered up into a tidy package that humbly I call the "Grouping of Greed Needs" or simply the "Greed Group." To develop the Greed Group, we must address first Maslow's "needs."

The Grouping of Greed Needs builds on Maslow's needs hierarchy. It incorporates his two highest needs, "Esteem," and "Self-Actualization," and adds a third, "Greed Above Need." The Greed

Group pays little consideration to Maslow's lower needs (physiological, safety, and love/belonging) simply because, at the executive level, these needs have been met, tampered with, and/or ignored.

And unlike Maslow's needs, the Greed Group is not a hierarchical association. Rather, the needs are "mutually inclusive." Each Greed Need is assimilated within all the other Greed Needs. They all mesh together with no need being more or less important than any of the others. In essence, by feeding on each other while at the same time supporting one another, all needs are equally essential.

The Grouping of Greed Needs

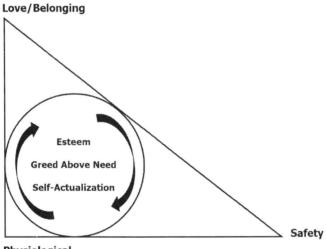

The Greed Group can be visualized as a self-contained sphere that rests upon (but does not incorporate) a base triangle of Maslow's lower needs. There is continual interaction between the needs within the sphere: Self-actualization feeds Esteem, which succumbs to Greed Above Need, which triggers Self-actualization, which fuels Esteem...and so on.

THE GREED GROUP – ESTEEM

> *Man will do many things to get himself loved;*
> *he will do all things to get himself envied.*
> **– Mark Twain**

Utilizing Maslow as a starting point, I have determined that the "Greed Group" incorporates "Esteem." The need for esteem is a requirement—corporate executives bathe in esteem. They are "royalty," after all, and as such expect and want to have all the power and trappings that go with it. It is an "entitlement attitude."

Dysfunctional executives, just like royalty, truly believe that inordinately they are superior beings compared to the "workers" who make up the rank-and-file of their corporation. By employing "royal rationalizations," [15] they have convinced themselves that they are "entitled" to wealth, prestige, and the deference and obedience of their subjects . . . I mean employees. After all, they're rich and the peasants are not (we all remember Leona Helmsly's infamous "little people" quote).

Medieval kings avowed that they were "ordained by God." The rest of us were merely God's undeserving servants. Executives believe that they are ordained by the gods of wealth and power. The rest of us are merely their undeserving servants.

Discounting Leona, most executives would never declare publicly that their rank-and-file employees were "inferior people." But I ask: when was the last time the CEO of your company "buddied up" to you to drink beer, swap dirty jokes, and throw some horseshoes?

COROLLARY: Dysfunctional executives believe that they are ordained by the gods of wealth and power. The rest of us are merely their undeserving servants.

---

[15] "Royal Rationalizations" are described in the next section.

THE GREED GROUP – SELF-ACTUALIZATION

My formula for success is rise early, work late, and strike oil.
– J. Paul Getty

Maslow's Self-actualization is also a Greed Need. Executives work hard; there is no denying that. It is not the effort they expend that is in question, but rather the inordinate recompense (compared to that of their employees) that is a cause for concern. This self-actualization—the undeniable fact that they do work hard—is important to them.

The hard work of self-actualization is a key rationalization executives utilize to justify their incomes. Later, we will learn that "rationalizations," along with the Id, are important factors that control executive Egos. Unfortunately, executives never give any consideration to the fact that almost everyone else works just as hard in their companies. Serfs are expected to work hard. It doesn't make them any less inferior.

THE GREED GROUP – GREED ABOVE NEED

Avarice has seized mankind that wealth possesses
them rather than they possess wealth.
– Pliny the Elder (23-79 AD)

There is only one more need in the Greed Group's association. I call it "Greed Above Need." It is defined as an almost irrational compulsion to gain more and more wealth, influence, and power with little or no consideration of any resultant consequences. Greed Above Need embraces "royal rationalizations," Esteem's entitlement attitude, and a concomitant lack of accountability. In effect, it boils down to this: "How much is too much?"

An executive possessed with Greed Above Need would answer smugly, "There is never too much." He (or she) already has a huge mansion, several palatial summer homes, a yacht, several super-cars, and a personal jet. He has also enough money to buy them all over again. But, still he wants more, and he will work diligently to gain more—often with little, if any, compassion or concern for the remaining members of the corporation—Greed Above Need.

THE GREED GROUP – PUTTING IT ALL TOGETHER

> *Do not spoil what you have by desiring what you have not.*
> **– Epicurus (341-270 BC)**

So, how does the Greed Group come about? That's where we bring in Freud.[16]

We have learned that Sigmund Freud believed an individual's personality was made up of three parts: the self-centered Id, the compulsive Superego, and the rational Ego. According to Freud, the Ego controlled the Id and Superego, keeping them in place. And most likely, for the majority of the world's population that is true.

However, I believe we have an anomaly with most members of a dysfunctional corporation's nobility. They have Egos and Superegos that are controlled by the Id. We know that the Id is selfish and uncaring. It demands to be satisfied immediately, and it has no contact with reality.

With the Id in control, the Superego is reduced to supplying hard work that is aggressive, compulsive, and sometimes (thanks to the Id) non-ethical in behavior. The Ego, rather than suppressing the Id, is controlled by it. Thus, the normally rational Ego becomes irrationally charged with gaining more and more of the things that the executive already has. It is an Id-controlled Ego that embraces Greed Above Need.

However, embracing Greed Above Need does require some form of "royal rationalization" that goes beyond the fact that the executive

---

[16] The Greed Group phenomenon applies not only to executives, but to individuals in certain select professions also where rationalizations, Ego, and Greed Above Need run rampant. Such professions are (not all-inclusive): Politicians, Automobile and Insurance Salesmen, Politicians, Lawyers, Politicians, Movie Stars, Politicians, Wall Street Brokers, Politicians, Professional Athletes, and Politicians.

is a hard worker. The Id may be controlling the Ego, but it has not overtaken it completely. If that were the case, the executive simply would be a sociopath—an uncontrolled and insatiable monster.

The Ego, therefore, despite the dysfunctional pervasiveness of the Id, does retain some control over the personality. And because of that, the executive must rationalize his gains, since it is only through rationalization that the executive can "con" his Ego into accepting his greed.

Unfortunately, rationalizations impact another factor, too; ethics. Once an executive begins to rationalize his or her actions, Greed Above Need will begin to suborn all ethical considerations. We'll cover this in more detail later when we talk about "Ethics—or the Lack Thereof."

ROYAL RATIONALIZATIONS

I can resist everything except temptation.
– Oscar Wilde

The Merriam-Webster dictionary defines "rationalize" as follows:

To attribute (one's actions) to rational and creditable motives without analysis of true and especially unconscious motives <rationalized his dislike of his brother>; broadly: *to create an excuse or more attractive explanation*

Dictionary.com defines "rationalize" as follows:

To ascribe (one's acts, opinions, etc.) to causes that superficially seem reasonable and valid but that actually are unrelated to the true, possibly unconscious and often less creditable or agreeable causes.

Rationalization is a major component of the famous Fraud Triangle proposed by the criminologist, Donald R. Cressey, in 1973. The triangle describes the three psychological elements a person must possess to commit fraud:

Opportunity, Motivation, and Rationalization.

As the powerful heads of major corporations, all executives possess the first element of the triangle, Opportunity. For dysfunctional executives, Motivation, the second element, has been replaced by "Entitlement." And the triangle's third element, Rationalization, is a major component of Greed Above Need, which, as we have learned, supports Entitlement.

THE FRAUD TRIANGLE

OPPORTUNITY

FRAUD

MOTIVATION

RATIONALIZATION

For the dysfunctional executive, "Entitlement" replaces "Motivation" on the triangle. Corporate nobles have convinced themselves that they are ordained by the gods of wealth and power, which makes them naturally more refined, better equipped, more intelligent, more capable, and more deserving than the average worker. And since they *are superior* to the average worker, they deserve—are entitled to—more money, more prestige, more power, more of everything.

This does not mean that an executive will commit fraud. But it does support his or her acceptance of the Grouping of Greed Needs. The executive's entire psychological structure is supported by "royal rationalizations" designed subconsciously to justify an entitlement attitude. As a result, the dysfunctional executive has no difficulty blurring that which is ethical with that which is not.

In his hypothesis, Cressey states that when people become "trust violators," a euphemism for "criminals," they apply to their conduct:

> ... *verbalizations [rationalizations] which enable them to adjust their conceptions of themselves as trusted persons with their conceptions of themselves as users of the entrusted funds or property.* [17]

---

[17] Donald R. Cressey, *Other People's Money* (Montclair: Patterson Smith, 1973) p. 30.

44

The actual rationalizations a dysfunctional corporate noble will use in defense of Greed Above Need are subject to the situation and the individual. In this respect there are practically an unlimited number of rationalizations or types of rationalizations that could be employed. Nevertheless, there are certain rationalizations that fall into recognizable patterns.

COROLLARY: Royal rationalizations impact the executive's ability to make prudent, ethical decisions. Royal rationalizations override logical and rational thinking, which, if carried to the extreme, could allow the noble to dispense with compassion, ethics, fairness, legality, and other such "mundane" concerns.

The subsequent list of "Classical Rationalizations" was taken from the following source:

http://www.ethicsscoreboard.com/rb_fallacies.html

Note: Rationalizations marked with an asterisk (*) are considered prime "Royal Rationalizations."

CLASSICAL RATIONALIZATIONS

Biblical – *"Judge not, lest ye be judged;"* and *"Let him who is without sin cast the first stone."* This type of rationalization is really a "cop out." It says to the world that it's ok for me to do this—even if it is wrong—because I know I am not perfect, and, unless you *are* perfect, you are not qualified to judge my mistake. Biblical rationalizations simply imply that actions taken can be judged only by "perfect" people.

The Golden Rationalization – *"Everybody does it."* This rationalization is structured around the flawed assumption that the ethical "value" of an act is directly proportional to the number of people who perform it. Simply put, if everybody does it, then it's alright for me to do it as well.

The Al Gore Misdirection – *"If it isn't illegal, it's ethical."* If they ever create an "Ethics Distortion Hall of Fame," Al Gore will be a charter member for defending his fundraising visit to the immortal Buddhist temple. Gore stated that, since "no controlling legal authority" had declared the visit illegal, it was not an ethical violation.

The *"Tit for Tat" Excuse* – Perceived to be valid if you can follow this logic: unethical behavior used to counter behavior that is bad or unethical somehow becomes ethical.

The Trivial Trap, Also Known as "The Slippery Slope" – *"An unethical act actually is ethical if it results in no tangible harm, i.e., "No harm; no foul."* Unfortunately, this allows the individual to embrace "the end justifies the means" paradigm as an ethical system.

The King's Pass – *"I am so important and I have done so much good that I should be excused this unethical behavior."* Undoubtedly, this is the quintessential royal rationalization. In essence, because of his or her exalted position, anything a corporate noble does, even if it is illegal, immoral, unethical, or fattening, is justified.

As an example, *The Washington Post* on February 25, 2007, ran the following headline, "Smithsonian Head's Expenses 'Lavish,' Audit Says." According to the article, written by James V. Grimaldi, the Smithsonian's top official, Lawrence M. Small, accumulated nearly $90,000 in unauthorized expenses from 2000 to 2005.

In smaller print, the *Post* reported, "Board Calls Small's Charges Reasonable." The Smithsonian's board of directors, according to the *Post*, ". . . accepted the [audit] committee's decision to dismiss the findings and defended Small's expenses."

Any "working Joe" with such "lavish expenses" would have lost their job and, most likely, been prosecuted.

The Saint's License – *"It's for a good cause."* This is an easily understood rationalization that probably has caused more death, destruction, and human suffering than any other.

*The Futility Illusion – *"if I don't do it, somebody else will."* I call this the "coward's plea." By justifying their lack of courage to say "no," this rationalization allows someone to do what they know is wrong. It is this rationalization that enables middle management to adopt the "tone at the top" and embrace "Corporate Greed."[18]

*Ethical Vigilantism – *This is the "I deserve it" or "they owe me" rationalization.* As an example, a person who was denied a promised raise begins to charge personal expenses to a company credit card.

Hamm's Excuse – *"It wasn't my fault."* This rationalization was named after American gymnast Paul Hamm, who refused to voluntarily surrender an Olympic gold medal that was awarded to him because of an official scoring error.

Hamm refused to return the gold medal, saying that it was the official's error, not his. Unfortunately, this rationalization confuses blame with responsibility. It basically says that a person does not have to fix an error he or she did not make.

*Comparative Virtue – *This rationalization embraces the "there are worse things" excuse:* telling a lie is not as bad as stealing something of value, which is not as bad as physically hurting someone, which is not as bad as selling military secrets to North Korea, etc. etc.

---

[18] "Corporate Greed" is greed that permeates the entire corporation. It is addressed in the next section.

> **COROLLARY:** Rationalizations are obstructions to clear, ethical thinking.

Here is another example of executive rationalization of Greed Above Need: *The Dallas Morning News* ran the following article on April 24, 2012:[19]

> *Dr. Kern Wildenthal, the chief fundraiser and former president of UT Southwestern Medical Center (UTSW), spent public money on personal travel abroad and showed "questionable judgment" in handling his expenses over the last several years.*

The article went on to say that, "Wildenthal resigned his position" and agreed to make "full restitution to UT Southwestern for reimbursements found to be inappropriate."

"Wildenthal will retain his tenured faculty position," UTSW spokesman Tim Doke said, and "his $950,000 salary would be adjusted to reflect his reduced roles."

When I read Doke's statement, I nearly choked. I mean, really, Wildenthal was making practically a cool million bucks a year and rationalized still a need to cheat on his expense reports!

Both Wildenthal and Small (the head of the Smithsonian who accumulated "lavish" unauthorized expenses) were extremely well-paid executives. And though we may never determine the actual rationalizations these men used, undeniably their cases present classic examples of "Greed Above Need."

---

[19] Sue Goetinck Ambrose and Reese Dunklin, "UT System report faults ex-UTSW chief Kern Wildenthal's spending," *The Dallas Morning News*, April 24, 2012, on-line at: http://www.dallasnews.com/investigations/headlines/20120424-ut-system-report-faults-ex-utsw-chief-kern-wildenthals-spending.ece (Accessed November 8, 2012).

LONG TIME A-COMING

Yabba dabba doo!
– Fred Flintstone (11925 BC)

Greed, Id, Ego, and their associated self-centered behaviors are not new to the corporate world or to human-kind in general, for that matter. These traits have existed since the first caveman whacked his neighbor on the head with a club, stole his hides, and then sold them to another caveman for a profit.

"I'll tell you what," he said no doubt to his freezing mark, "I'll sell you these hides for your hunting spear, your two daughters, and an option on the next mammoth you kill."

Of course, the first neo-executive would have conditions—the "fine print," if you will. "If you don't kill a mammoth within the next two suns, you gotta give me the hides back and I'll give you your spear back; but I keep your daughters."

The unfortunate mark had no choice: he had to accept—he was freezing to death. And the fact that "two suns" most likely was not enough time to build another spear and find and kill a mammoth was part of the Neanderthal exec's cunning plan. From the very beginning, his goal was to get the hides back, while keeping the daughters, of course (who didn't mind one bit because he supplied them with furs). As the world's first executive, he didn't need the spear.

Nor is serfdom something new. The ancient Greeks considered it a crime to kill a fellow citizen. Killing a slave, however, merited no mention, let alone any punishment. The Romans, who were merely a bunch of misplaced Greeks after all, continued the concept. Roman slaves were property. They could be beaten, tortured, or killed without consequence.

At the birth of our great nation, Thomas Jefferson wrote so beautifully: "We hold these truths to be self-evident, that all men are created equal, that they are endowed by their Creator with certain unalienable Rights, that among these are Life, Liberty and the Pursuit of Happiness."

As I said, these are beautiful words. However, what we fail to recognize is the simple fact that Mr. Jefferson himself was a rich, capitalist landowner who owned hundreds of slaves but, within his lifetime, freed only two.

EXAMPLES OF EXECUTIVE GREED ABOVE NEED

Be fearful when others are greedy, and
be greedy when others are fearful.
– Warren Buffett

In a previous section, we discussed the greed-grabbing of people like Dr. Kern Wildenthal and Lawrence Small, both highly-compensated executives who rationalized somehow that they needed to cheat on their expense reports. But, padding expense reports is "small potatoes" compared to what other executives have been doing.

On August 31, 2011, Reuters reported the following:[20]

Twenty-five of the 100 highest paid U.S. CEOs earned more last year than their companies paid in federal income tax, a pay study said. It also found many of the companies spent more on lobbying than they did on taxes.

Further, Reuters reported that Representative Elijah Cummings (D–Maryland) asked, in a letter to the Committee on Oversight and Government Reform chairman, Darrell Issa (R-California), "to examine the extent to which the problems in CEO compensation that led to the economic crisis continue to exist today."

Cummings asked "why CEO pay and corporate profits are skyrocketing while worker pay stagnates and unemployment remains unacceptably high." He questioned also "the extent to which our tax code may be encouraging these growing disparities."

GENERAL MOTORS: I've already given you the example of GMC's CEO, Rick Wagoner, who was fired in an unprecedented move by President Obama. Wagoner headed GM for a period of nine unsteady years that were characterized by multiple failures. He ignored the trend toward lighter, more fuel efficient vehicles, he ran

---

[20] Nanette Byrnes, "Some U. S. firms paid more to CEOs than taxes: study," *Reuters*, August 31, 2011, on-line at: http://www.reuters.com/article/2011/08/31/us-usa-tax-ceopay-idUSTRE77U0KW20110831 (Accessed November 3, 2012).

up massive debt, and he championed the Pontiac Aztek, which I believe is no doubt the ugliest car ever to set wheels on America's roadways (apparently everyone else agrees with me because the car didn't sell). In fact, *TIME* Magazine rated the 2001 Aztek as one of "The 50 Worst Cars of All Time."[21]

Nevertheless, before he was canned, Wagoner continued to receive lucrative pay raises and incentives. Reuters reported the following:[22]

> *General Motors Corp (GM.N) Chief Executive Rick Wagoner's salary and other compensation rose 64 percent in 2007 to about $15.7 million, mainly due to option grants, according to a proxy filed on Friday.*

And finally, though he was "officially barred" from receiving a severance package, ABC News reported on March 30, 2009:[23]

> *Rick Wagoner will leave his post as CEO of bailed-out General Motors with a $20 million retirement package, the company's financial filings show. Although the Treasury Department has barred GM from paying severance to Wagoner or any other senior executive, Wagoner is eligible to collect millions in retirement benefits from his former employer, according to the documents reviewed by ABC News.*

---

[21] Dan Neil, *TIMELists*, on-line at: http://www.time.com/time/specials/2007/article/0,28804,1658545_1658544_1658540,00.html (Accessed November 3, 2012); *TIME* and Dan Neil, Pulitzer Prize-winning automotive critic and syndicated columnist for the Los Angeles *Times*, looked at the greatest lemons of the automotive industry.

[22] David Bailey, "GM CEO's compensation jumps 64 percent in 2007," *Reuters*, April 25, 2008, on-line at: http://www.reuters.com/article/2008/04/26/businesspro-gm-ceo-dc-idUSN2534738420080426 (Accessed November 3, 2012).

[23] Michelle Leder and Justin Rood, "PAYDAY: GM's Rick Wagoner Drives Away with $20M Retirement," *ABC The Blotter*, ABC News, March 30, 2009, on-line at: http://abcnews.go.com/Blotter/story?id=7208201&page=1 (Accessed November 3, 2012).

BANK OF AMERICA: In 2007, Kenneth Lewis earned nearly $100 million as CEO of Bank of America, even as he was leading the Bank to its eventual collapse and subsequent absorption by Merrill Lynch. According to Robert B. Reich in his book, *After-Shock* (page 33):

To spend it all, Lewis would have had to buy $273,972.60 worth of goods and services every day that year, including weekends. If he had devoted twelve waking hours a day to the task, he'd have had to spend $22,831 every hour, $380.52 every minute.

LEHMAN BROTHERS: Another great greed-grabber was Richard Fuld, CEO of Lehman Brothers. By 2007, the year prior to the firm's calamitous downfall because it couldn't pay its bills, Fuld had collected salary and stock options to the tune of $500 million in total compensation.

Director, an on-line magazine at http://www.director.co.uk, reported on November 10, 2010:[24]

Between 1993 and 2007, Fuld reportedly received nearly half a billion dollars in total compensation. In 2007 alone, he earned a total of $22m, including a base salary of $750,000, a cash bonus of $4.25m and stock grants of $16m. Fuld was chairman of the board of directors and CEO. He was king.

WASHINGTON MUTUAL (WaMu): Washington Mutual Bank protected its nobility after booking unprecedented losses in 2007. The problem was brought about by the fact that the bank had relaxed lending requirements for its home mortgages. Termed "sub-prime," these loans were meted out to borrowers who, under normal circumstances, never would be qualified to obtain a mortgage.

---

[24] Jamie Oliver and Tony Goodwin, "The king of sub-prime," *Director*, on-line at: http://www.director.co.uk/ONLINE/2010/11_10_dick-fuld-how-they-blew-it-lehman.html (Accessed November 3, 2012).

Why would WaMu do this? Well, a number of factors were involved, including governmental directives—begun within the Clinton administration—to relax lending requirements, thus allowing more Americans to own homes. Unfortunately, Clinton's directive was just a door opener for greed.

Sub-prime borrowers are charged much higher interest rates, which translate into higher revenues, which in turn translate into bigger bonuses for the nobility. When times are good, this does not pose a problem for the nobles. Unfortunately, the economy began a downturn. It started as a trickle, but as more and more of the sub-prime borrowers began to default on their loans, the trickle turned into a raging flood. The net result was a rash of huge loan write-offs.

No less than two major mortgage lending firms went under during the landslide, and a large number of banks were forced to take huge losses for 2007. WaMu was one of them. CNBC reported that WaMu booked a whopping $1.87 billion loss in the 4th quarter of 2007, which triggered a $2.19 decline per diluted share in the bank's stock.[25]

The results of this loss, as well as further losses repeated in the following two quarters, forced WaMu to close offices and reduce staff. On December 11, 2007, the *Los Angeles Times* ran the following headline: "Mortgage losses prompt WaMu to cut more jobs."[26] In the ensuing article, the *Los Angeles Times* reported that WaMu was terminating over 3,000 employees:

> *The savings and loan, one of the largest U.S. home mortgage lenders, said a sharp downturn in demand for home loans was*

---

[25] "WaMu Reports $1.8 Billion Loss, Misses Forecasts," CNBC.com, January 17, 2008, on-line at:
http://www.cnbc.com/id/22712225/WaMu_Reports_1_87_Billion_Loss_Misses_Forecasts (Accessed November 3, 2012).

[26] "Mortgage losses prompt WaMu to cut more jobs," *Los Angeles Times*, December 11, 2007, on-line at: http://articles.latimes.com/2007/dec/11/business/fi-WaMu11 (Accessed November 3, 2012).

forcing it to eliminate 2,600 mortgage and 550 corporate support jobs, or 11% of its total staff, and close 190 of 336 mortgage offices.

However, on March 5, 2008, just a few months after the huge layoffs, *The Wall Street Journal* reported that the bank's board voted to award bonuses nevertheless to the Corporation's top executives. In the article, reporters Valerie Bauerlein and Ruth Simon stated that the board of Washington Mutual inc.:[27]

...has set compensation targets for top executives that will exclude some costs tied to mortgage losses and foreclosures when cash bonuses are calculated this year.

The move, approved last week and disclosed in a securities filing late Monday, essentially shields the pay of chairman and chief executive of the thrift, Kerry Killinger, and more than 100 other executives from the continuing mortgage fallout.

WaMu declared that the huge mortgage write-offs were a "one-time" exceptional situation. It would not be fair to the executives to consider it when the bonus payments were meted out. Unfortunately, this same "fairness" was never a consideration when over 3,000 of the company's employees were notified of their layoffs.

UNITED AIRLINES: *Airwise News* reported the following on March 17, 2005:[28]

---

[27] Valerie Bauerlein and Ruth Simon, "WaMu Board Shields Executives' Bonuses," *The Wall Street Journal*, March 5, 2008, online at: http://online.wsj.com/article/SB120468286834912411.html (Accessed November 3, 2012).

[28] "Bankrupt United Airlines Paid CEO Bonus," *Airwise*, March 17, 2005, on-line at: http://news.airwise.com/story/view/1111053350.html (Accessed November 3, 2012).

55

Bankrupt United Airlines paid its top executive a bonus of over USD$366,000 last year as the company sought salary and other concessions from union workers ....

Let me restate this to ensure I understand it correctly: The top executive's incompetence led the firm into bankruptcy, and to help remedy the situation, he asked employees to accept pay cuts "and other concessions." Nevertheless, he managed to rationalize accepting, as a reward, a bonus of $366,000. Did I get that right?

BORDERS: Apparently United Airlines is not the only bankrupt firm that is willing to reward its royalty with bonuses for their abject failure. On March 26, 2011, *The Wall Street Journal* reported in an article by Peg Brickley:[29]

Book retailer Borders Group Inc., which is shuttering hundreds of stores in a bid to stay alive, is seeking bankruptcy court approval to hand out as much as $8.3 million in executive bonuses, including nearly $1.7 million to President Mike Edwards.

If this doesn't present a classic example of "royal rationalizations" and Greed Above Need, I don't know what does. The company is insolvent—facing bankruptcy, shutting down stores, terminating employees—and it wants to pay humongous bonuses to its royalty!

Am I the only one who sees the logical disconnect here? Border's royal handouts make the United Airlines bonus cited above look like "peanuts."

ENRON AND WORLDCOM CORPORATIONS: Indeed, the largest bankruptcies in history were brought about by the Greed, Egos,

---

[29] Peg Brickley, "Boarders Seeks To Hand Out $8.3 Million In Bonuses," *The Wall Street Journal*, March 26, 2011, on-line at: http://on-line.wsj.com/article/SB10001424052748704474804576222642969830886.html (Accessed November 3, 2012).

unethical, and illegal activities of the executives in these two huge companies. Without going into detail, since it would take hundreds of volumes (and hundreds of volumes already have been written), the losses were piling up and being covered up into the billions, while the executives paid themselves huge salaries, bonuses, and stock options.

Enron: In February 2002, *TIME* Magazine reported:[30]

> *[Kenneth] Lay, who helped found Enron in 1985 and became its CEO, has received about $200 million in salary, stock and other compensation from Enron since 1999. He enjoyed privileges rare even for top CEOs, such as the $7.5 million revolving credit line Enron extended him.*

TIME also reported that Jeffrey Skilling, former Enron CEO, sold off about $20 million in Enron stock between January and August 2001, just before the Securities Exchange Commission opened an official inquiry on October 24, and Enron filed for bankruptcy on December 2, 2001.

WorldCom: Seen as one of the success stories of the 1990s, WorldCom filed the largest Chapter 11 bankruptcy in history, listing $41 billion in debt. On July 11, 2002, CNN *Moneyline* reported:[31]

> *Fired WorldCom Chief Financial Officer Scott Sullivan is claiming that ex-CEO Bernie Ebbers knew about the company's questionable accounting.*

Ebbers, whose $10 million bonus came on top of a salary package that made him one of the highest paid executives in the world, was

---

[30] Eric Roston, "The Enron Players," *TIME* Magazine, February 4, 2002, on-line at: http://www.time.com/time/magazine/article/0,9171,1001767,00.html (Accessed November 3, 2012).

[31] "WorldCom ex-CFO: Ebbers Knew," CNN Money, July 11, 2002, on-line at: http://money.cnn.com/2002/07/11/news/companies/worldcom/index.htm (Accessed November 3, 2012).

convicted of leading an $11 billion accounting fraud that caused the eventual breakdown of the firm.

Every negative adjective you can think of applies in the cases of Enron and WorldCom, from lying and unethical conduct, to misfeasance, misrepresentation, and outright theft. Although thousands of employees eventually would lose their jobs, pensions, and 401(k)s, the executive nobility awarded themselves millions in bonus payments and then relinquished stock for millions more just before the bottom fell out.

And finally . . . .

With corporations struggling to stay afloat, unemployment at an all-time high, and an economic crisis threatening the very existence of America's capitalist system, the following report by Joann S. Lublin appeared in *The Wall Street Journal* on March 17, 2011:[32]

> *CEO bonuses at 50 major corporations jumped a median of 30.5%, the biggest gain in at least three years, according to a study of the first batch of corporate CEO pay disclosures by consulting firm Hay Group for The Wall Street Journal.*

Ms. Lublin subsequently reported in *The Wall Street Journal* on May 9, 2011:[33]

> *The median value of salaries, bonuses and long-term incentive awards for CEOs of 350 major companies surged 11% to $9.3 million, according to a study of proxy statements conducted for The Wall Street Journal by management consultancy Hay Group.*

---

[32] JoAnn S. Lublin, "Executive Bonuses Bounce Back," *The Wall Street Journal*, March 17, 2011, on-line at: http://on-line.wsj.com/article/SB10001424052748703818204576206903329068840.html (Accessed November 3, 2012).

[33] JoAnn S. Lublin, "CEO Pay in 2010 Jumped 11%," *The Wall Street Journal*, May 9, 2011, on-line at: http://on-line.wsj.com/article/SB10001424052748703992704576307332105245012.html

ETHICS – OR THE LACK THEREOF

Ethics: the Rodney Dangerfield of Professional Responsibilities.
– David Cotton, CPA

It is not my intention to present a definitive article on ethics. Nevertheless, the above listed corporate disasters, lack of executive accountability, and growing disparity in wealth distribution make it obvious that, woefully, ethics has been ignored at the top of America's major corporations. Of course, the mere fact that, in actuality, no one can agree on the meaning of the term presents somewhat of a dilemma.

I looked up the definition of "ethics" both on-line and in various dictionaries and business pronouncements. No two publications provided the same definition. Nor did any two publications approach the "concept of ethics" in the same way. Nevertheless, our unwavering reference, Merriam-Webster, defined ethics as follows:

> *1 plural but sing or plural in constr:* the discipline dealing with what is good and bad and with moral duty and obligation

> 2 a set of moral principles: a theory or system of moral values <the present-day materialistic *ethic*> <an old-fashioned work *ethic*> —often used in plural but singular or plural in construction <an elaborate *ethics*> <Christian *ethics*>

I like the part about ethics being a "theory," since a theory often is untested or untried—and I maintain that ethics certainly have been untried at the tops of America's corporations. But, for the purposes of this primer, I settled finally on the definition of ethics I liked best. It is taken from the following site:

http://www.more-for-small-business.com/definition-of-ethics.html

> *Ethical business behavior may be defined by law, but it also can be defined by business leadership. Generally speaking an*

action or choice can be considered ethically correct if it's honest, fair, supports a beneficial outcome for both parties, and generally enables the overall corporate image and vision.

What I liked immediately about this definition is that it started with "ethical business behavior ... can be defined by business leadership" and ended by stating that ethical behavior "enables the overall corporate image and vision." This definition not only fits my thesis exactly, but it was the only definition I could find that addressed corporate image.

My supposition simply is this: the "tone at the top" can make or break a corporation. If corporate royalty steers the firm in an ethical direction, it will run ethically at all levels. However, if the tone at the top directs the company in an unethical direction, "Corporate Greed" will permeate all levels of the firm.

When considering the frauds, cons, misappropriations, misdirection, deceit, and greed that occurred within the examples cited in this book, we can accept as a fact one common characteristic that was displayed in all cases: there was a lack of ethics. And we have discovered already that a lack of ethics goes hand-in-hand with the development of Greed Above Need. The failures of Enron and WorldCom, the bonus payments to WaMu and Borders executives, and the outrageously high income of a failing Lehman Brothers' president are examples of egregious Greed Above Need.

I submit respectfully that the players in these economic tragedies, thanks to their Greed Above Need, rationalized their gains while displaying blatantly a disregard for the inevitable consequences. And respectfully I submit that ethics, because of those rationalizations, never entered into the arena.

COROLLARY: It is the "tone at the top" that can make or break a corporation.

THE COMPONENTS OF ETHICS

I contend that ethics is a daily struggle; it is a constant struggle. But, what are the factors that comprise "ethics" or make up "ethical considerations?" While, in actuality, the following qualities may not define ethics, they are at least components of ethics. They were developed from my research into the subject. Consequently, they were compiled from terms that were employed by a variety of sources. Nevertheless, I believe them to be a basic, but fairly descriptive, listing of fundamental requirements.

- Honesty
- Integrity
- Accountability
- Responsibility
- Selflessness
- Respect
- Fairness
- Competence
- Loyalty
- Diligence

There is nothing difficult about "ethics". . . except *having* ethics, of course. The concept is quite simple actually: Ethics is the above listed qualities combined with common sense, a value-set that does not ignore right from wrong, and established volitions that allow you to act appropriately on that sense of right vs. wrong.

If you possess these attributes, you should have no problem making ethical decisions. Obviously, the converse applies also: if you are missing any of the above qualities, no doubt you are rationalizing away your ethical considerations, and "Greed Above Need" becomes the value-set of the day.

COROLLARY: There is nothing difficult about "ethics". . . except *having* ethics, of course.

I have perused a number of books, texts, and manuals that concern ethics. Every one of them stated (in some manner or other) that ethics derives from making the right decision when faced with a dilemma or conflict of interests. That decision-making requires the decision-maker to have the right mix of the qualities listed above. It also requires that the decision-maker be free from rationalizations.

Given what we've learned so far, finding a lack of ethics at the top of a dysfunctional corporation is not so surprising actually. Executives in these corporations are in positions of power and prestige — positions that often lend themselves to unethical decisions because in the executives' minds, thanks to their Greed Above Need, the decisions are not unethical. Executives are dysfunctional when they do not possess the right mix of ethical qualities and are not free from rationalizations.

Dysfunctional corporate royalty subscribes to an "entitlement attitude." Ripe with rationalizations, the nobles conclude that they've done a lot of good for their corporations (even if they haven't); so, it is only right that the corporations do a lot of good for them.

Quite simply: if you have no ethics, *everything* is ethical.

PART II

THE DYSFUNCTIONAL PRINCIPLES OF THE CORPORATION

IN SUMMATION

The dysfunction of a corporation in part lies with the skewed set of values and volitions that emanates from the very top of its hierarchical pyramid.

Greed, a lack of ethics, and Id-controlled Egos are basic—and faulty—building blocks that support the dysfunctional corporate structure.

PART III

THE MEMBERS OF THE CORPORATION, BEING HUMAN, ARE DYSFUNCTIONAL BY DEFINITION

THE MEMBERS OF THE CORPORATION ARE DYSFUNCTIONAL BY DEFINITION

Criminal: A person with predatory instincts who has not sufficient capital to form a corporation.
— Howard Scott

So far, we have discussed two of the three causal determinants of a dysfunctional corporation: Structure and Principles. Structure, the first determinant, fosters dysfunction because the corporation is a feudal institution that channels the wealth, prestige, and power of the company into the hands of the chosen few.

The second determinant, Principles, begins at the very top of the corporate hierarchy. This determinant describes how executive royalty's Greed Above Need, royal rationalizations, and lack of ethics have led many large corporations to ruin.

Now it's time to discuss the third determinant, the "Human Members of the Corporation."

All corporations are composed of humans (a quite obvious observation) and are loaded with managers, directors, supervisors, section leaders, and so forth. The question becomes: Where do these people, the so-called "Middle Management," fit within the corporate hierarchy? Are they included with the executives or are they considered to be part of the corporate peasantry? Most importantly, can they, too, succumb to the Greed Group?

BusinessDictionary.com defines Middle Management as follows:

. . . managers who head specific departments (such as accounting, marketing, production) or business units, or who serve as project managers in flat organizations. Middle managers are responsible for implementing the top management's policies and plans and typically have two management levels below them. Usually among the first to be slashed in the 'resizing' of a firm, middle management constitutes the thickest layer of managers in a traditional (tall pyramid shaped) organization.

The BusinessDictionary.com definition (above) supports the fact that, so far as the corporate nobility are concerned, Middle Management is lumped in with the serfs. A division director may be paid better than most employees, and he or she even may receive a bonus. But, the director's income will not come even close to the perks and payouts that the company's royalty receive. And, of course, he or she can be terminated just like any other non-royal personage.

Nevertheless, it is the members of a company's middle management who are key to the acceptance and promotion of "Corporate Greed."

"Corporate Greed" is the "bleed-down" of Ego, Greed Above Need, and a lack of ethics from upper tiers to middle management and even certain rank-and-file employees, who will embrace whatever socio-political concepts they believe will foster their successful rise within the corporation.

In a dysfunctional corporation, Greed, Ego, and the Greed Group are not limited to just the executive royalty. Employees, most notably those who are "wanabe executives," most certainly will emulate "the tone at the top." They can and will embrace the credo of Ego and Greed if they believe that it will be their ticket to advancement. As a result "Corporate Greed," which embraces "royal rationalizations" and the Greed Group, most certainly will "trickle down" through the management strata of a dysfunctional corporation.

DYSFUNCTIONAL CORPORATE EGOS

To understand dysfunctional corporate egos, we must accept a set of assumptions or suppositions that define the dynamics of corporate personalities within a dysfunctional corporation—and to some extent, within normal or non-dysfunctional corporations also. These assumptions are:

- There is only one class of greed (all-consuming)
- "Corporate Greed" permeates the company's feudal culture
- The greed is a function of rationalized, Id-controlled Egos.

Once we accept these assumptions, we can separate Corporate Egos into three dysfunctional classes. These classes are not mutually exclusive. The three classes are:

- Super-Successfuls
- Ingratiating-Sycophants
- Superior-Inferiors.

COROLLARY: Corporate Greed and Corporate Egos are not mutually exclusive: all Dysfunctional Corporate Egos embrace Corporate Greed.

Super-Successfuls

Egotism -- usually just a case of mistaken non-entity.
— Barbara Stanwyck

First are the Super-Successfuls. These are people who are driven to succeed by an almost all-consuming work ethic. Life is defined by work; their only reason for living is to work. They arrive in the office early and stay late, sometimes working into the wee hours of the morning. I have known executives who even slept in their offices overnight in order to continue with a project. In reality, the great majority of these people utilize the corporation to compensate for terrible home lives. I call this class of employee "Super-Sucks."

Working with or for Super-Successfuls is nothing less than a nightmare. Their superiority (within their own minds) is a given. They are always pushing for more output, and they can be demanding, demeaning, and demoralizing. A Super-Suck will treat those who are higher in rank with deference. Conversely, co-workers and underlings will be treated not quite as highly as dirt. Super-Sucks are anal-retentive, self-centered, and convinced that they—and only they—are competent enough to really know what's going on.

A key Super-Suck trait is their inability to be wrong. If a Super-Suck makes a mistake, he or she will never own up to it. Rather, a true Super-Suck will maintain always that someone else was at fault, often coming up with Machiavellian explanations to shift the blame to another. And here is a word of caution: Never *ever* make the mistake of proving that a Super-Successful indeed was wrong. They will never ever forget it. They *will* get even, and the consequences for you will not be pretty.

Just remember when dealing with Super-Sucks: unless you "outrank" them, you are considered in their eyes to be far less than human.

Ingratiating-Sycophants

Cleverness is not wisdom.
– Euripides (480-406 BC)

Next on the list are the Ingratiating-Sycophants, a.k.a. "Brown-Nosers," "Ass-Kissers," or "AKs." The sad thing is that these people are so stereotypical, it's almost criminal. At a minimum, there is at least one AK in any reasonably sized department.

AKs operate under the premise that the best way to get ahead is to get the boss to see just how great they are (compared to the mediocrity of their co-workers). They do this by being noticed and by making the boss believe that they think exactly as he or she does.

Ass-Kissers carry networking to its farthest extreme. Their game is to be "noticed;" that is, they always want the light to shine on them. They constantly "yes" the boss and engage him or her in "small talk;" they socialize with management outside of the office; and they "jump in," never disdaining to knock a co-worker aside, whenever there is a chance to hog the limelight.

Although, in actuality, Ass-Kissers may not look down on their co-workers or consider them to be inferior, they do maintain a somewhat snobbish or superior attitude. And certainly, they don't want their co-workers getting in their way.

You have to be careful around Ass-Kissers. You may think they are being nice to you because they like you. Unfortunately, they are only interested in two things: (1) obtaining something from you that they may be able to pawn off to the boss as their own; and (2) discerning a weakness that they may be able to use against you (to their advantage) in the future.

Yep, Ass-Kissers will be your buddy in one instant and then in the next they (a) will steal something you have done and claim it as their own, (b) will denounce you to the boss if they believe it will enhance their own status, or (c) will do both (a) and (b) above. The fact that Super-Successfuls are intolerable only emphasizes the fact that Ingratiating-Sycophants are deplorable.

Superior-Inferiors

> *You cannot have a proud and chivalrous spirit*
> *if your conduct is mean and paltry.*
> *– Demosthenes (384-322 BC)*

My discussion of Super-Successfuls and Ingratiating-Sycophants really didn't touch upon the subject of competency. This is because the level of competency for those Egos is not what matters. Whether they are competent or not, Sucks and Kissers have decided to employ methods other than their actual abilities to achieve advancement.

The situation is different, however, for Superior-Inferiors, simply because they are the only class of corporate Ego that may be truly incompetent. Superior-Inferiors are people who, for whatever reason, really don't have what it takes to succeed and, thus, overcompensate with pompous arrogance, negative aggression, and overpowering superiority: Simply, I call these people "bastards."

When dealing with Superior-Inferiors, understand that they will "one-up" you constantly in order to deflect your ability to determine just how much they do not know. It's simply "the best defense is a good offense" type of disposition, and to protect their lack of ability, they will employ it arrogantly and aggressively.

Superior-inferiors will attack negatively everything anyone else does. In a nutshell, their game is to enhance their stature by chipping away at yours. These bastards will focus unrelenting attention on even unimportant trivialities if necessary to lessen the possible impact a competent co-worker or underling could make.

Never make a mistake in front of a Superior-Inferior because, no matter how trivial it is actually, the bastard will "work it to the hilt." In no time at all, you might find yourself being counseled about your attitude, work product, conduct, and/or competency.

A really good Superior-Inferior will possess all the aspects of an Ingratiating-Sycophant. Thus, like the Ass-Kissers, they defer to those who outrank them, consider their peers to be inferior obstacles, and have no compunction against stealing something someone else has done and claiming it as their own. In fact, since they do very little real work on their own, stealing the work of others is a mainstay of their survival.

Unlike Ass-Kissers, however, Superior-Inferiors never will pretend to be nice to you in order to get what they want. Rather, right from your first meeting, a bastard will make it very clear to you that he or she is smarter, more capable, and just generally a better person than you ever will be.

Also unlike AKs, the level of negative aggression they display towards you will correspond directly to their perception of your level of competency. Thus, where an Ass-Kisser will criticize your work (to management) only when they believe it will enhance their stature, a bastard, on the other hand, will denigrate you constantly, because he or she believes that the more you shine the more it detracts from his or her status. It's simply this: the better they believe you to be, the worse they need to make you seem.

We're talking about dysfunctional personalities here, folks. Superior-Inferiors go way beyond the basic greediness and self-centered Egos of the other classes. Bastards indeed are the worst of a bad bunch of apples.

And finally, there is a fourth class actually . . .

Grinders

Your average parking meter makes more a day than I do.
– Al Bundy

The vast majority of a corporation's employees fall into a fourth class of corporate Ego. These are the "Grinders;" that is, people who work the daily grind assiduously in order to eke out their meager existences.

Unlike the other classes, Grinders have Egos that actually control their Ids and Superegos. They are the true producers in any organization, and it is only because of this fourth class that corporations manage to survive at all. Unfortunately, all the other classes conspire effectively to conceal this fact.

Grinders want to do a good job and want to get ahead. But a Grinder will never backstab someone else or kiss the derrière of his or her boss in the process. Rather, Grinders want to be measured solely on the merits of their "work."

Unfortunately for Grinders, management rarely uses "merit" and "work" to recognize or reward employees (other than for minor promotions or pay raises). Rather, "merit" and "work" are only applied by management in antithetical situations. It is when these criteria are "absent" that they are used; and then only to reprimand, demote, or terminate employees.

In other words, a diligent, loyal, and productive worker may receive a whopping 2% - 3% pay raise at performance review time (assuming times are good and there is some money left over after corporate royalty received already 200 - 400 times that amount). And a Grinder eventually may rise up in the ranks from employee to team lead, supervisor, or even manager.

But a loyal, diligent, productive worker will *never* advance into the realm of corporate royalty. It just won't happen, no matter how competent he or she may be. The converse, however, is true. Should an employee fail to perform or make a mistake on the job, they will be disciplined, demoted, or, if deemed a serious transgression, "advanced" into the realm of the unemployed.

Grinders are the true losers in the corporate world because they are outgunned by the other classes. Unfortunately, it is because dysfunctional corporate nobility fall invariably within those other classes that, as a class, Grinders truly never will succeed.

MISSING THE POINT

Remember, it's pillage first, then burn.
- Viking Proverb

It all boils down to this: Grinders, Super-Sucks, AKs, and bastards interact continually with each other in the mystifyingly intricate and absurdly repetitive dance of the everyday working world. And each day they make ignominious political-sociological moves in voracious, self-serving attempts to "get ahead."

Unfortunately, they are making the wrong moves. I submit respectfully that there are no successful dancers here—every employee class is missing the point.

Employees believe that to be recognized as successful within their companies, they are expected to produce something. They must make a widget, deal with a customer, process paper (electronically or physically), generate a management report, or any one of a number of different tasks. I contend that this is not the true measure of success.

I stated earlier that production, merit, and work may be used as reasons to demote or terminate (when they are lacking), but when present, never are used as criteria for significant advancement. This still holds true.

The truly successful employee is not the employee who improves a product, nor is it the employee who improves customer service. And, ass-kissing or back-stabbing notwithstanding, it is not the employee who will "kill" to get ahead. Although these things may garner some small recognition and minor advancement, they are not the criteria that will propel an employee into the elite ranks of corporate royalty.

COROLLARY: In democracy, your vote counts. In feudalism, your count votes. In a corporation, money counts and you have no vote.

To advance in any corporation, you must do one thing – and only this one thing counts. To advance in any corporation, you must increase revenues. Nothing else matters! Simply put, "Ya gotta bring in da bucks." You may kiss up to the boss, and he may like you even. But, if you don't bring in *mucho dinero*, don't expect to go very far.

Obviously, if you can increase revenues, you put more money in your boss's pocket, and his boss's pocket, and so on, right up the chain. And if you bring in a "substantial" amount of bucks, nothing else matters. There will be no need for ass-kissing, you won't have to be super aggressive, you won't have to display a superior demeanor, and you won't even have to work very hard.

I guarantee it: you could be obnoxious and dress like a harlequin, but if you put a couple million bucks in the CEO's pocket, he'll treat you like a prodigal son. Of course, on the other hand, if the money stops, your favored status will stop with it.

To prove my point, when I worked for Arthur Andersen (long before its ultimate demise), all employees—from partners[34] to lowly grunt auditors—were subject to a severe dress code. Not only did we have to be neatly groomed, but also we had to be appropriately dressed. This meant that in the dead-heat of summer, when it was 95 degrees Fahrenheit with 95% relative humidity, I was forced to wear a jacket and tie to the office.

Arthur in Philadelphia in those days was huge, employing in its center-city office over 1,000 people and occupying four full floors of a Market Street skyscraper. Obviously, all kinds of people (all appropriately dressed) were moving in and out of the offices all the time.

However, I noticed one person who worked in the office occasionally: this guy was an anomaly. He was a partner (I knew this because he had a partner's office), but he had long hair that he wore in a ponytail, and he wore blue jeans and an open-collared

---

[34] "Partner" in an accounting firm is the equivalent to "executive" in a corporation. Partners are the accounting firm's nobility.

shirt (no tie) in the office. I never met the man, nor did I see him very often, but the few times that I did see him, he was dressed in blue jeans and an open collared shirt. I never saw him wearing a suit.

I discovered eventually that he was a partner indeed. I discovered also that he was responsible for the second-largest account in Arthur's inventory (the largest being, sadly, Enron). Through family connections, he alone was responsible for bringing millions of dollars of revenue a month into the Philadelphia office—nearly more than all the other partners combined.

Because of the revenue he generated, he worked his own hours and wore whatever he wished when he visited the office. Blue jeans notwithstanding, I submit respectfully that he could have sauntered into the office wearing a diaper and no one would have said a disparaging word.

COROLLARY: The employee who truly will succeed in a corporation is the employee who generates substantial revenues (brings in the bucks).

PART III

THE DYSFUNCTIONAL HUMAN MEMBERS OF THE CORPORATION

IN SUMMATION

The dysfunction of a corporation in part lies with the willingness of employees to accept "Corporate Greed." Emulating the tone at the top is psychologically common, since employees can and will embrace the credo of Ego and Greed if they believe that it will be the ticket to advancement.

Inherent human dysfunction is a basic—and faulty—building block that supports the dysfunctional corporation.

PART IV

OUT OF CONTROL

OUT OF CONTROL

Who are you going to believe, me or your own eyes?
- Groucho Marx

We've talked about corporate structure, greed, the problems associated with the Id and the Ego, royal rationalizations, and the inherent human weaknesses that drove executive nobility into some of the world's largest financial fiascos. However, while contemplating these fiscal disasters, there are two very important and decidedly perplexing questions that we have not addressed yet:

(1) Where were the financial controls that should have prevented these disasters?
(2) For Heaven's sake, where were the auditors?

Obviously, frauds and failures of huge magnitudes would occur rarely if sufficient financial controls and independent monitoring were in place. In all of the corporate disasters we have discussed, there was a clear breakdown in internal controls as well as some form of audit failure.

COROLLARY: Frauds and failures of huge magnitudes would occur rarely if sufficient financial controls and independent monitoring were in place.

OVERRIDDEN INTERNAL CONTROLS

The breakdown in financial controls is rather easy to understand. Quite simply, they were overridden at the highest levels. Royalty can do that, since no one will dispute the CEO's or CFO's decision to book something regardless of its conformity, or lack thereof, with GAAP.[35]

---

[35] GAAP – Generally Accepted Accounting Principles – These are the governing principles that assure (supposedly) all accounting transactions are true and proper.

At the risk of repeating myself, I will restate briefly that for the royalty in a dysfunctional corporation, the Id forces the Ego to rationalize the all-consuming need for gaining wealth, power, and prestige, a.k.a., "Greed Above Need." It is these very rationalizations that deter or cloud the executives' clear or sound ethical thinking. So, of course, these corporate heads were ready and willing to break the rules.

AUDIT FAILURES

Audit failures, on the other hand, are a little more complex because auditor ethical deficiencies came about for different reasons. To begin with, ethics always was considered to be a technicality for auditors. In fact, it wasn't until 2001 that the majority of states even paid much attention to ethics for CPAs. Up to that time, the accounting profession considered CPA's, by definition, to be ethical beyond any question or doubt.

In 2002, Jesse F. Dillard and Kristi Yuthas published, "Ethical Audit Decisions: A Structuration Perspective," in the *Journal of Business Ethics*. In that article, they state:[36]

> *The public accounting profession has long relied on a reputation for integrity and veracity to justify its societal, and market, relevance.*

So, for over a century, certified public accountants were considered to be at the pinnacle of the ethical hierarchy.[37]

Then the bubble collapsed: WorldCom, under the very noses of its auditors, capitalized operating expenses in order to hide $13 billion in losses. Enron, with the approval of its audit firm, hid massive

---

[36] Jesse F. Dillard and Kristi Yuthas; "Ethical Audit Decisions: A Structuration Perspective;" *Journal of Business Ethics*, Volume 36, Numbers 1-2, 2002.
[37] We can contrast this with politicians, who for untold millennia always have been considered to be in the very basement of the ethical hierarchy.

debt and losses under the technical guise of special purpose entities. And Arthur Andersen, at the time one of the country's most prominent accounting firms, shredded work papers and other documents in anticipation of being subpoenaed.

There appeared to be a sudden shortage of ethics, practically overnight, and by 2002 most state boards of accountancy responded by requiring mandatory ethics training as a condition for CPA licensing—as if taking a course would convert someone from an unethical to an ethical person. Nevertheless, it meant now that accountants or CPAs no longer were presumed to be "ethical beyond a doubt." The paradigm had changed; they now must be *trained* to conduct themselves in an ethical manner.

Unfortunately, requiring CPAs to take an ethics course is nothing more than mere window dressing. The accounting profession's client-accountant relationship structure is the real ethical dilemma auditors face. This dilemma is in the form of a conflict of interest: Fees.

Under our current audit model, a publicly traded firm (which means any firm that has common stockholders) must undergo an annual financial audit by an independent public accounting firm. The accounting firm is paid a fee for conducting this audit, and in the case of very large corporations, this could be a very large fee.

Because of this fee-based relationship, I contend that every financial audit project presents a conflict of interests for the auditors that impedes their independence. To put it in layman's terms, auditors always face a dilemma: Should they "bite the hand that feeds them?"

This is the situation that existed between Enron and its "independent" auditors. At the time of Enron's demise, Arthur Andersen performed the annual financial audit, which generated millions of dollars in revenue for the accounting firm. In addition, Arthur was providing consulting services to the huge corporation, which generated also millions of dollars in revenue.[38]

---

[38] The practice of providing consulting services to clients subsequently was restricted by Section 201 of The Sarbanes-Oxley Act of 2002 (PL 107-204).

Is it any wonder that the auditors would fail to report material accounting errors or omissions? Arthur was in the midst of an ethical dilemma: Should they report the gross misstatements, thus risking the loss of a major client and millions of dollars in revenue, or should they go-along with the scam, thus protecting the huge revenue stream they obtained from their client?

And should Count Dracula switch to drinking milk instead of blood? We all know which answer Arthur chose. Nevertheless, the American Institute of Certified Public Accountants (AICPA) has determined that auditing for a fee is NOT a conflict of interests.[39]

COROLLARY: The accounting profession's client-accountant relationship structure poses an ethical dilemma. This dilemma occurs in the form of a conflict of interest: Audit Fees.

---

[39] Author's Note: In Part VII, we will revisit the client-accountant relationship during a discussion of Public Law 107-204, The Sarbanes-Oxley Act Of 2002.

PART V
A DIFFERENT VIEW

A DIFFERENT VIEW

OFFICE WISDOM: When executives talk of improving quality, they are never talking about themselves.

My observations in this book are based on years of experience in the corporate world (in both high- and low-level positions). I've stocked shelves in a supermarket, loaded trucks in a warehouse (as a union worker), pushed paper in an insurance company, and managed employees for a bank and a CPA firm. Eventually, I became the director of audit in a large engineering firm (in which I reported to the board of directors). In addition, I have spent an untold number of hours doing research in libraries and on the internet. So, I should know what I'm talking about (whether I really do or not is a matter of interpretation and conjecture).

I am sure that I will be criticized for being far too harsh in both my highly opinionated observations of the dysfunctional corporation and my cynicism concerning corporate leaders. I accept this criticism, but in my defense, I must point out that I tried actually to find authors who would present an opposing view.

Strangely enough, finding articles that contradicted my thesis was no easy task. It seems, in actuality, that most writers agree with me, although they tended to temper their pronouncements in order to be less controversial, less direct, and certainly less obnoxious.

Nevertheless, I prevailed. I found an author who disagreed with me completely. So, now, in what you may perceive to be rather a lame attempt to provide a more balanced treatise, I am going to supply an opposing viewpoint.

In his book, *Building Social Business*, Muhammad Yunus states:[40]

The biggest flaw in our existing theory of capitalism lies in its misrepresentation of human nature. In the present

---

[40] Muhammad Yunus, *Building Social Business*, (New York, Public Affairs, a member of the Perseus Group, 2010), page xv.

interpretation of capitalism, human beings engaged in business are portrayed as one-dimensional beings whose only mission is to maximize profit. Humans supposedly pursue this economic goal in a single-minded fashion.

You could say that, with this paragraph, Mr. Yunus challenged my thesis beautifully. Indeed, I have presented corporate royalty in a one-dimensional manner. My whole premise is that *all* executives desire wealth, which equates to power, which equals prestige; and I contend that is the dysfunctional corporate royalty of the world that subscribes fully to the one-dimensional Greed Group. As the renowned American poet, Ralph Waldo Emerson, said, "A man is usually more careful of his money than he is of his principles."

Muhammad disagrees with me (and I assume Mr. Emerson) completely. He goes on to state that humans derive happiness "from many sources, not just from making money." He believes that the existing theory of capitalism ignores or denies any other aspects of life, such as "political, social, emotional, spiritual, environmental, and so on." Accordingly, Muhammad believes that there are two kinds of businesses: "one for personal gain, another dedicated to helping others."

It is in this second business, which he names "social business," that—these are his words, mind you—"an investor aims to help others without making any financial gain himself." I can't help but wonder what Mr. Yunus would say if he were asked to consider the swindles and scams perpetrated by people such as Carlo Ponzi, Bernie Madoff, Bernie Ebbers, or Jeffrey Skilling.

In brief, Muhammad Yunus starts out with a correct premise, at least where the corporate nobility is concerned. I agree with him when he says the biggest flaw in current capitalistic theory is the fact that it is one-dimensional. But my agreement ends there.

The basic premise of this primer is that corporate executives are deemed dysfunctional when they are entirely self-centered and conduct their business (and personal) affairs without compassion, ethics, or integrity. It is these executives who personify the archetypical, entitled corporate nobility.

Driven by Greed Above Need, dysfunctional corporate nobility has only one goal: to maximize personal wealth, influence, prestige, and power. To this end, indeed, they may not be one-dimensional; nevertheless, that one aspect of their personalities most definitely dominates all others.

Therefore, I cannot accept the idea that corporate royalty can contemplate doing something for the downtrodden peasantry. Royalty, in fact, secretly holds the peasants in contempt. After all, it is decreed by the gods of wealth and power that nobles are "entitled" and, thus, superior to the peasantry.

The dysfunctional corporate executive believes that employees should be thankful for having a job. And if any serfs should be terminated (i.e., laid-off) . . . well, that's really not of much concern to the members of the nobility, because they are miles above such mundane matters. Besides, the decreased salary and benefits costs to the company will have a positive effect on the nobles' contracted bonus computation formulas—always good news for royalty, regardless of the impact on peasants. And are layoffs really so bad? I mean, the peons have unemployment insurance, right?

Now, you could oppose my view by stating that, on many occasions, corporate nobles have contributed large sums to charities and other humanity-driven type organizations. You could . . . . But, I would counter your argument by pointing out that such contributions are induced by tax write-offs, and usually are well publicized, which serves to increase the individual noble's prestige and esteem.

The proof is in the pudding. If corporate royalty had any compassion for the peasants who worked for them, there rarely would be lay-offs. Any executive who makes millions of dollars could prevent layoffs merely by holding down his or her pay.

For example: an executive who receives a bonus of a million dollars could prevent, by forgoing such bonus, the layoffs of approximately 17 people (assuming an average salary of $40,000 with another $20,000 in benefits per person). No executive ever made that sacrifice on the occasions when I was laid off, nor have I ever heard tales of such altruistic nobility.

Actually, in this treatise I have proven the opposite. I have cited examples where thousands of employees were laid off or accepted pay cuts, while executives received lucrative bonuses (see Washington Mutual, United Airlines, WorldCom, Borders, and Enron above).[41]

---

[41] There is an interesting aside here: When I showed a very rough draft of this book to a (rather successful) friend, he became incensed. He defended layoffs heatedly by stating that a corporate executive is responsible to stockholders for showing a profit, which may mean a necessary need to cut costs -- thus layoffs. I countered by saying that an executive bonus increases corporate costs regardless of the number of peons terminated. He replied that a bonus is a corporate obligation required by a contract between the executive and the corporation. I concluded my argument by saying: "Whether contractually mandated or not, the acceptance of a bonus when employees are laid off is elitist, self-serving, ethically inappropriate, and morally heinous."

A DIFFERENT VIEW – Part 2

What's the use of happiness? It can't buy you money.
– Henny Youngman

I want to emphasize once again that most companies (along with the executives who lead them) deal ethically with the business world and care about the people who work for them. The truly dysfunctional corporation is a rare entity. However, I must emphasize also that no executive or corporation is completely free from dysfunction—that would contradict the basic laws of nature.

I've already told you that I had a varied and interesting career. In my time, I've worked for several corporations, and I would have no problem defining one or two of them as dysfunctional. But, I have to admit that I did work for a corporation that was remarkably non-dysfunctional.

I was the Director of Internal Audit for CDI Corporation from the mid-1980s to the mid-1990s. At the time, CDI, an engineering firm headquartered in Philadelphia, had revenues of about $1.5 billion and maintained operations in nearly every state as well as several countries in Europe. In my capacity as chief auditor, I reported directly to the Audit Committee of the Board of Directors.

During my employment with CDI, I was impressed with the ethics and integrity displayed by the top executives within the firm. The Chief Executive Officer (who was also Chairman of the Board), the CFO, and several other executive officers were individuals who, although they worked diligently, were not Id-controlled, nor had they succumbed to the Greed Group.

In a nutshell, CDI was run effectively by a small cadre of executives who displayed honesty and integrity in their business dealings throughout my years of employment with the company.

Now, you're probably thinking that the CDI example does not support my dysfunctional corporation thesis—and you would be right. However, please remember that truly dysfunctional firms are the exception, as the cliché goes, not the rule. CDI may not support my thesis, but it does not negate it either. And it does support the following assertion that I made earlier:

The "tone at the top" can make or break a corporation. If corporate royalty steers the firm in an ethical direction, it will run ethically at all levels.

I cite the example of CDI because my experience with this company supports my contention that the principles of a corporation will determine the functioning of the entity at all levels. Those principles start at the very top. And at the top, CDI was an ethically-run corporation.

As a result, most of the operations within the corporation functioned with minimum dysfunction. This does not mean there were no problems. There were cases of theft and fraud; not *every* executive was free from Greed Above Need; and not every decision was free of ethical challenges. But, I reiterate: The laws of nature dictate that no individual or corporation can be perfect.

The point I wish to make is that CDI's top executives were not blinded by all-consuming greed and chose to run the business with a sense of ethics and integrity. The executives wanted to make money, of course. They worked hard; and they were well paid. The key was that, lacking Greed Above Need, they did not have to rationalize unethical behavior in order to succeed.

COROLLARY: There are large corporations with executives who are not Id-controlled. These corporations deal ethically with the business world and care about the people who work for them.

PART VI

A BRIEF SYNOPSIS

A BRIEF SYNOPSIS

Lack of money is the root of all evil.
– George Bernard Shaw

We're at that point in this primer where I should recount—that's recount, not recant—our lessons learned so far. First, we learned that the modern corporation isn't very modern at all.

The corporation is a medieval institution, wherein corporate royalty reap all the rewards while holding the power of economic life or death over their worker subjects. Although we have been led to believe that a corporation's mission is to build something or provide a service, we learned from this primer that its true and actual mission is to increase the wealth, prestige, and power of its corporate nobility.

We learned next that two basic principles govern the operation of all dysfunctional corporations. Those principles are Greed and Ego. The greed is all-consuming because the corporate leaders have succumbed to the Grouping of Greed Needs. This means that the Egos of corporate leaders are controlled by their Ids . . . and I'm sure that if Sigmund Freud could read this he would begin rolling over in his grave right about now.

And lastly, we learned that, being human, the corporation's royalty and employees by definition are dysfunctional.

If you have gotten this far, you should pat yourself on the back, because truly you now have learned the real meaning of a corporation:

Corporate perks: Royalty gets 'em; the peasants don't!

PART VII
SO, WHAT DO WE DO ABOUT IT?

SO, WHAT DO WE DO ABOUT IT?

The greater the difficulty, the more the glory in surmounting it.
— Epicurus (341-270 BC)

So, what do we do about it? How do we combat Greed Above Need—which stems from a basic human desire for wealth, prestige, and power? What can we do to prevent future dysfunction in our corporate entities?

Are there answers to these questions? Well, I'm not sure. But, I do know that as a result of the corporate meltdowns described within this primer, America has begun adopting an approach designed to prevent and/or combat the dysfunctional corporation. Consequently, several major actions did take place during the first decade of the new millennium.

I believe the three most important actions taken during the period 2000 to 2010 are:

1. Establishment of the Corporate Fraud Task Force
2. The Sarbanes-Oxley Act of 2002
3. Subtitle E—Accountability and Executive Compensation (Sections 951 through 956) of the Dodd-Frank Wall Street Reform and Consumer Protection Act of 2010.

THE CORPORATE FRAUD TASK FORCE AND SUBSEQUENT INTERAGENCY FINANCIAL FRAUD ENFORCEMENT TASK FORCE

On July 9, 2002, in what only can be termed a "knee-jerk" reaction to the corporate accounting scandals that shook investor confidence, President George W. Bush issued Executive Order 13271. The order established "The Corporate Fraud Task Force."

It was the Corporate Fraud Task Force working under the US Department of Justice that pushed through the successful prosecutions of key executives such as Bernie Ebbers and Jeffrey

Skilling. Also, it was a key player in the demise of Enron's accounting firm, Arthur Andersen.

The Corporate Fraud Task Force was replaced on November 17, 2009, when President Barack Obama issued Executive Order 13519, by which he established the new and improved "Interagency Financial Fraud Enforcement Task Force."

According to the official Justice Department news release, the purpose of the new and improved task force was "to strengthen efforts to combat financial crime."[42] The news release continued by saying that various departments and agencies within the Federal Government

> . . . will work with state and local partners to investigate and prosecute significant financial crimes, ensure just and effective punishment for those who perpetrate financial crimes, address discrimination in the lending and financial markets and recover proceeds for victims.

> The task force, which replaces the Corporate Fraud Task Force established in 2002, will build upon efforts already underway to combat mortgage, securities and corporate fraud by increasing coordination and fully utilizing the resources and expertise of the government's law enforcement and regulatory apparatus.

PUBLIC LAW 107-204, THE SARBANES-OXLEY ACT OF 2002

Not to be outdone by the President, Congress enacted the Sarbanes-Oxley Act of 2002 (PL 107-204) on July 30, 2002. Commonly known as "SOX," the law resulted from an "after-the-fact" reaction to the Enron, WorldCom, and other major corporate accounting scandals that I have mentioned in this book (along with

---

[42] The Justice Department news release can be found at: http://www.justice.gov/opa/pr/2009/November/09-opa-1243.html (Accessed November 14, 2012).

other corporate failures that I have not cited, such as Tyco International, Adelphia, and Peregrine Systems).

These scandals ruined the lives of rank-and-file employees (whose jobs were lost and whose pension and 401(k) plans were devastated), cost investors billions of dollars, collapsed share prices of the affected companies, and shook public confidence in the nation's securities markets. And they occurred because of the "royal-rationalized" Greed Above Need of each corporation's top executives.

A decade after its enactment, Sarbanes-Oxley is being debated still. To this day, experts and analysts have not reached any common conclusions regarding the perceived benefits and costs of SOX. The bill's many opponents claim that it has damaged America's competitiveness internationally, especially against foreign financial service providers, by introducing an overly complex regulatory environment into U.S. financial markets.

In addition, opponents claim there is no clear indication that SOX has deterred fraud within America's corporate community. On December 22, 2008, Michael S. Malone in a *Wall Street Journal* editorial stated:[43]

> *The new laws and regulations have neither prevented frauds nor instituted fairness. But they have managed to kill the creation of new public companies in the U.S., cripple the venture capital business, and damage entrepreneurship.*

On the other hand, proponents of the measure claim SOX is a "godsend," since it has improved the veracity of corporate financial statements and, thus, bolstered the confidence of fund managers and other investors. A company's CEO and CFO, under Section 302 of Sarbanes-Oxley, now are required to take unequivocal ownership of their financial statements, which means when the proverbial you-

---

[43] Michael S. Malone, "Washington Is Killing Silicon Valley," *The Wall Street Journal*, Opinion, December 22, 2008, on-line at: http://online.wsj.com/article/SB122990472028925207.html (Accessed November 3, 2012).

know-what hits the fan, they can attempt no-longer to play the "I know nothing" card as a defense.

This was not the case prior to SOX. Therefore, financial and industry experts point out that SOX has resulted in more accurate and reliable financial statements.

Finally, SOX supporters claim that the law addressed the auditor conflict of interest problem, since Section 201 prohibits auditors from having lucrative consulting agreements with the firms they audit. Personally, I believe that precluding accounting firms from "lucrative consulting agreements" only partially resolves the problem. SOX falls short because, as I have stated before, it does not address the problem of audit fees.

Obviously, eliminating consulting projects removes an important impairment to auditor independence. However, the failure to address the conflicts of interest accounting firms experience when they perform annual financial audits for a fee leaves another important impairment staunchly in place.

To ensure you understand, let me reiterate the situation briefly. Currently, the Securities and Exchange Commission (SEC) requires a publicly traded company to publish an "independently audited" annual financial report in which the auditors express an opinion on the soundness and accuracy of the firm's published financial statements. The "official" term that accounting firms use to describe the financial statements is "present fairly."

If there is sufficient disclosure, reasonable detail, and an absence of bias in the firm's financial statements, the audit report will state that the financials "present fairly the firm's financial position, results of operations, and cash flow." This terminology has been used in financial reporting since 1932.

Under the current model, the accounting firm is paid a fee by the corporation for this service. Prior to the enactment of SOX, accounting firms provided consulting services, too, as a result of their relationships with their clients, also for a fee. Accountants are no longer permitted to consult for the firms they audit;

nevertheless, I contend that the audit for a fee scenario, which is permitted still, presents a significant impairment to the independence of accounting firms.

Unfortunately, even though many alternative auditing scenarios have been proposed since the great corporate meltdowns of the early 21st century, the AICPA maintains still that the audit of corporate financial statements for a fee is NOT a conflict of interest.

I disagree with the AICPA. Accounting firms are not independent when performing financial audits for a fee. And of the many scenarios that have been put forward, the one I favor follows:

The SEC should require publicly-traded firms to publish annual "insured" or "bonded" financial reports. According to this model, an accounting firm would audit the company's financial statements and express an opinion thereto. The difference here is that the company being audited would not purchase the audit directly from the accounting firm.

Rather, the publicly-traded company would purchase financial statement insurance from an insurance provider. The audit would be conducted by whichever accounting firm the insurer has hired, thus resolving any conflicts of interest between the accountants and the audited firm.

There are benefits to this type of arrangement:

- The insurer would hire or retain accounting firms to perform financial audits of its clients
- The auditors are neither chosen nor paid by the audited company, so the accounting firm is truly independent, and there is no conflict of interest
- The insurer, to protect its interests, actually would WANT the auditors to report all material deficiencies they find; the accounting firm would not face the dilemma of "biting the hand that feeds it"
- The company's increased cost for insurance may be offset to some degree by reduced audit fees based on economies of scale experienced by the insurer

- The shareholding public would be protected to some extent from corporate failures, because the audited statements would be "insured;" the level of insurance possibly could affect the financial value of the company's stock (the higher the insurance, the safer the investment).

COROLLARY: Accounting firms are not independent when performing annual financial audits for a fee.

PUBLIC LAW 111-203, DODD-FRANK WALL STREET REFORM AND CONSUMER PROTECTION ACT (JULY 21, 2010)

Throughout this primer, I have argued against the exorbitant compensation packages corporate royalty receive; and you would think that, logically, I would argue equally fervently for some form of regulatory control. But, this is not the case.

I am totally opposed to government control over executive compensation; however, my opposition does not apply to public disclosure of executive compensation. On July 21, 2010, Congress approved the Dodd-Frank Wall Street Reform and Consumer Protection Act of 2010 (usually referred to as "Dodd-Frank").

The bill was directed mainly towards security trading on Wall Street (hence the "Wall Street Reform and Consumer Protection" reference in its name). But, also it has provisions designed to control executive pay—not by government decree—but rather by corporate governance and public disclosure.

Subtitle E—Accountability and Executive Compensation (Sections 951 through 956), of the act requires the Securities and Exchange Commission to adopt regulations that:

- Require companies ". . . to conduct a separate shareholder advisory vote to approve the compensation of executives . . . ." and, in certain circumstances, to conduct a separate shareholder advisory vote to approve the golden parachute compensation arrangements.

- Require national securities exchanges to prohibit listing issuers that do not possess independent compensation committees.
- Require additional disclosures with respect to executive compensation in the following areas:
  o The relation of executive compensation actually paid and the financial performance of the issuer
  o The median annual compensation of all employees of the issuer excluding the chief executive officer
  o The annual total compensation of the chief executive officer
  o The ratio of chief executive officer compensation to the median annual compensation of all employees of the issuer excluding the chief executive officer

The "additional disclosures" requirement, especially the last bullet, which requires disclosure of a comparison of CEO compensation to rank-and-file employee compensation, was opposed strongly by corporate lobbyists who wanted to block the rule. Nevertheless it was enacted and took effect in April 2011.

Some of the requirements in Dodd-Frank already had been in place. For example: the corporate Form 10K always reported CEO compensation.[44] However, this information *never* was emphasized, nor was it compared to rank-and-file compensation. Plus, the disclosures always were buried within the voluminous pages of the report, forcing the unaccustomed reader to wade through pages and pages of financial data and other information.

And there are shortfalls in Dodd-Frank. For example: the shareholder approval of CEO compensation, though required, also is

---

[44] A **Form 10-K** is an annual report required by the U.S. Securities and Exchange Commission (SEC) that gives a comprehensive summary of a public company's performance. Although similarly named, the annual report on Form 10-K is distinct from the often glossy "annual report to shareholders," which a company must send to its shareholders when it holds an annual meeting to elect directors (though some companies combine the annual report and the 10-K into one document).

"nonbinding." This is unfortunate. In effect, the control does not rest with shareholders directly (a position that I believe Congress evaded purposely), but rather with the legislature's supposition that compensation committees would try to avoid a potential "no" vote by stockholders. Such a vote, even though non-binding, would make it difficult for the compensation committee to support its proposed executive pay package.[45]

Since the regulations for Dodd-Frank only took effect in 2011, it remains to be seen if they will engender the desired results. Even though it is not perfect, at least in the area of executive compensation, Dodd-Frank definitely is a step in the right direction.

IMPORTANT DISCLAIMER: Dodd-Frank is a huge bill, the bulk of which deals with matters other than executive compensation.

I am not familiar with these other areas of the bill; therefore, I cannot and do not applaud or decry their effectiveness.

MY UNDERSTANDING AND APPROVAL OF DODD-FRANK PERTAINS TO THE FOLLOWING SECTION OF THE BILL ONLY:

Subtitle E: Accountability and Executive Compensation (Sections 951 through 956).

---

[45] I believe Congress avoided the shareholder approval of executive pay for purely personal reasons. Think about it. If shareholders are given the right to control executive salaries, then, logically, shouldn't voters be given the right to control their representatives' pay? Congressional pay currently is approved by the members of Congress themselves. No senator or congressman wants to put his salary in the hands of his constituents.

AND FINALLY . . . THE REAL PROBLEM

We make a living by what we get, but we make a life by what we give.
– Winston Churchill

The real problem, so far as this primer is concerned, is that no person, institution, or government can combat effectively "royal rationalizations" and Greed Above Need. We can take a tougher approach as America appears to have done in the aftermath of the great corporate meltdowns. We can try to control greed through laws, regulations, and task forces. We can prosecute greed when corporate royalty oversteps its bounds. We can attempt to educate people about the building blocks of greed, as I have done in this primer.

Albert Einstein said, "It is easier to denature plutonium than to denature the evil spirit of man." I hope that the passage of Sarbanes-Oxley and Dodd-Frank will help to allay some of the dysfunctions that are plaguing American corporations. I hope, too, that executive greed can be mitigated somewhat—not through government control—but instead through increased internal control, public disclosure, and stockholder overview of the enormous amounts CEOs and other royalty receive.

I've indicated that Subtitle E of Dodd-Frank is too new to gauge adequately any measure of its failure or success.

I contend that the jury is still out concerning the Sarbanes-Oxley Act, even though SEC Chairman Christopher Cox stated in 2007:

> *Sarbanes–Oxley helped restore trust in U.S. markets by increasing accountability, speeding up reporting, and making audits more independent.*[46]

---

[46] Greg Farrell, "SOX Law Has Been a Pretty Clean Sweep." *USA Today*, July 30, 2007, on-line at: http://www.usatoday.com/money/companies/regulation/2007-07-29-sarbanes-oxley_N.htm (Accessed November 3, 2012).

And, except for an article in *The Economist* dated January 14, 2005, I have heard very little about the Interagency Financial Fraud Enforcement Task Force since its inception (as the Corporate Fraud Taskforce) in 2002 and re-invention in 2009. According to that article, the Corporate Fraud Task Force[47] is running out of companies to prosecute—whether this means that SOX is working or not was not divulged. The article states:[48]

...its future role will be one of fraud prevention now that prosecutions have been brought in the big cases.

Little since has stirred media attention beyond the Interagency Financial Fraud Enforcement Task Force's crackdown on financial company fraud relating to residential mortgage-backed securities.

So, in conclusion, will this tougher approach have any effect on dysfunctional executives and corporations? The best answer I've seen so far appeared in the previously cited article in *The Economist*:[49]

The real problem is that it is hard to judge the efficacy of measures to clean up corporations. At least until the next spate of scandals comes to light.

Finally, to sum it up, we should reflect upon our inherent values and volitions to determine an answer to the following question.

Ask yourself: If you were in a position to make millions and millions of dollars as a powerful, highly-compensated executive, would you

---

[47] The article predates establishment of the new and improved Interagency Financial Fraud Enforcement Task Force.

[48] "Trials and Errors," *The Economist*, January 14, 2005, on-line at: http://www.economist.com/node/3572974?zid=292&ah=165a5788fdb0726c01b1374d8 e1ea285 (Accessed November 5, 2012).

[49] "Trials and Errors," *The Economist*, January 14, 2005, on-line at: http://www.economist.com/node/3572974?zid=292&ah=165a5788fdb0726c01b1374d8 e1ea285 (Accessed November 5, 2012).

fall into the trap of an Id-controlled Ego, rationalize your decisions, and con yourself into accepting Greed Above Need?

I have pondered this question throughout the process of writing this book. I decided finally that for me the answer is three-fold: (1) I'm not sure; (2) certainly it could be "Yes;" and (3) most assuredly, I would love to be in a position to find out.

Perhaps the American writer and Nobel laureate William Faulkner stated it best when he said, "I never know what I think about something until I've read what I've written on it."

ADDENDUM - THE CORPORATION

I think it's wrong that only one company makes the game Monopoly.
— Steven Wright

There are three major forms of business organization, each with several different legal and operating variations: sole proprietorship, partnership, and corporation. The form of business organization we are concerned with here is the corporation.

According to The Merriam-Webster Dictionary, "corporation" is a noun with the following definitions:

1: a group of merchants or traders united in a trade guild *b*: the municipal authorities of a town or city
2: a body formed and authorized by law to act as a single person although constituted by one or more persons and legally endowed with various rights and duties including the capacity of succession
3: an association of employers and employees in a basic industry or of members of a profession organized as an organ of political representation in a corporative state

The Encyclopedia Britannica defines "corporation" as follows:

Corporation, specific legal form of organization of persons and material resources, chartered by the state, for the purpose of conducting business.

According to the Britannica, a corporation is distinctive, when compared with the other two major forms of business organizations, because it incorporates features that make it more advantageous to large-scale business operations. These features include:

Limited liability, which protects capital investors who will not subsume losses greater than their investments;

Transferable shares, which allows ownership in the entity to be transferred readily without any major corporate restructuring;

117

<u>Juridicial personality</u>, which means the corporation itself assumes standing as a legal "person." As such, the company can sue and be sued, hold property, and make contracts;

<u>Indefinite duration</u>, which simply means the life of the entity can extend past that of any of its incorporators or stockholders.

WORKS CITED

Abraham H. Maslow, *Motivation and Personality* (Pearson, 3rd Edition, 1997)

Donald R. Cressey, *Other People's Money* (Montclair: Patterson Smith, 1973)

Jesse F. Dillard and Kristi Yuthas, "Ethical Audit Decisions: A Structuration Perspective," *Journal of Business Ethics*, Vol. 36, No. 1-2 (2002): 49-64

Robert B. Reich, *After-Shock: The Next Economy and America's Future* (New York: Alfred A. Knopf, 2010)

Muhammad Yunus, *Building Social Business: The New Kind of Capitalism that Serves Humanity's Most Pressing Needs* (New York: Public Affairs, 2010)

ABOUT THE AUTHOR

Your whole life to date has been training for right now.
– Robert Asprin

Lawrence (Larry) Gambone has a Master's degree from Rutgers University and is a Certified Public Accountant. He is a veteran, having served with the US Army during the Vietnam War.

Born in Camden, New Jersey, Larry grew up in the "wilds" of South Jersey, and has lived in such exotic places as Europe, Hawaii, Guam, and Washington D. C. Larry is 2nd generation American, the product of Italian immigrant families that "came over by boat" to Ellis Island in the very early years of the 20th Century. He believes it is this humble upbringing that gives him his "down-to-earth" outlook on life, the economy, and the nation.

Why Corporations Fail is Larry's second book. The first, written with Louis C. Gilde, is entitled *The Dilution of America*.

Currently, Larry lives in Texas with his wife and, most importantly, near his grandchildren.

Made in the USA
Charleston, SC
18 April 2014